1991

THE ENGLISH HOUSE

James Chambers

THE ENGLISH HOUSE

WITH ILLUSTRATIONS

SELECTED AND CAPTIONED

BY ALAN GORE

W·W·NORTON & COMPANY

New York   London

© 1985 Alan Gore and James Chambers
First American edition 1985
All rights reserved.

Library of Congress Cataloguing in Publication Data

Chambers, James.
The English house.

Includes index.
1. Architecture, Domestic—England. I. Title.
NA7328.G66   1985   728′.0942   85–4833

ISBN 0-393-02241-2

W. W. Norton & Company, Inc.,
500 Fifth Avenue, New York, NY 10110
W. W. Norton & Company, Ltd.,
37 Great Russell Street, London WC1B 3NU

Printed in Great Britain

1 2 3 4 5 6 7 8 9 0

Contents

List of Illustrations

The illustrations in this book were selected and captioned by Alan Gore, who is the architectural adviser and writer of the Thames Television series *The English House.*

Picture research by Julia Brown.

The publishers are grateful to the following copyright owners and photographers for permission to reproduce the illustrations. All possible care has been taken to trace and acknowledge the sources of illustrations. If any errors have accidentally occurred, however, we shall be happy upon notification to correct them in any future editions of this book.

7

9

Introduction

ENGLAND contains a greater variety of domestic architecture than any other country in the world. Although some countries have had as many traditional regional styles or have been blessed with as many different natural materials, the English have built new houses in new styles more often, and of those styles that prevailed during the nine hundred years since they were last invaded, examples of almost all have survived. On the whole, the English variety is due to little more than accidents of history and the fact that England, although part of Europe, is also part of an off-shore island. The English developed a large number of their styles in isolation, from time to time they absorbed or adapted contemporary European styles as well, and they even adopted one European style long after it had fallen from fashion elsewhere, with the result that it evolved uninfluenced thereafter into a uniquely English version. During the sixteenth century, when the architects of Catholic Europe were following the Italian Renaissance, the newly Protestant builders of England were developing another style of their own, fusing their traditional Gothic architecture with a few second-hand elements of Renaissance decoration which had been brought to them from Protestant Flanders and Germany. At the beginning of the eighteenth century, when Rococo was the height of fashion in Europe, the English were at last building in the style of the Italian Renaissance.

By no means all of their domestic architecture is good, but the English did have one great stroke of luck. They achieved their best at a time when more men than ever before could afford to live in new houses. During the eighteenth century, when rapid growth in the agricultural economy was followed by the Industrial Revolution, the Classical ideal of the Renaissance spread throughout England as 'The Rule of Taste'. Lesser men followed the examples of the great aristocratic mansions, and in applying the Classical principles of symmetry and proportion to smaller houses, cottages and terraces alike, they created the style now known as 'Georgian'.

Unfortunately, however, the English Classical tradition contained the seeds of self-destruction. Even at the outset, the architects of the great mansions were not just copying the style of the Renaissance, they were also drawing on the Roman buildings which had inspired it. As time passed, they turned more and more to the models of the ancient world, and by the end of the eighteenth century, when they were reaching back beyond Rome to Greece, their archaeological curiosity, combined with romanticism, had led them to examine the Gothic buildings of their own more recent past. In 'The Battle of the Styles' that followed, Classical domestic architecture was defeated, and 'The Rule of Taste' was overwhelmed in fanciful and nostalgic confusion.

But the houses that have survived from the different centuries are much more than examples of changing fashions. They are also important historical records. Rich men build symbols of their power and poor men build the best they can. The houses that they leave behind record their aspirations and their social and economic progress, and above all they record a changing way of life. At the beginning of the Middle Ages the manor houses of England and northern France were very similar in plan; towards the end of the Middle Ages their plans were different, not because of any radical changes in style, but because of the different ways in which their owners used them. The formal sequences of rooms in the early eighteenth-century plans and the huge isolated servants' wings of the nineteenth century reflect the manners and attitudes of their times, just as the Classical proportions of Georgian houses and the Gothic extravagance of Victorian fantasies reflect the tastes and values of their builders. Houses, like all other architecture, are images of the society that built them. Throughout the centuries they have altered as much with custom as with fashion.

Essentially, therefore, this book is a story. It is the story of a changing society, and of the evolution within that society of what Le Corbusier described as 'a machine for living in'.

CHAPTER 1

A Form of Shelter

THE first houses in the country now known as England were built less than a hundred years after the birth of Christ. They were large, dignified, comfortable houses, similar in basic design to the houses in the rest of the Roman Empire. They had brick walls, frescoes, colonnaded courtyards and heating ducts beneath mosaic floors. But, unlike their Mediterranean counterparts, they did not survive to become the models from which subsequent houses evolved. During the Dark Ages they were destroyed by invaders who built in the style of their Teutonic homelands, reverting to the simple materials that had been used before the Romans came. It was to be more than a thousand years before England saw their like again; and it is one of history's many ironies that when the English began to build houses with as much symmetry and elegance, they turned for their example to Italy, to the descendants of the very people whose houses their ancestors had demolished.

The earliest inhabitants of Britain slept under the stars during the summer and lived in caves during the winter, covering the entrances with heather and branches. For their first free-standing shelters, they used the same heather and branches to build no more than little open-ended tents. It was not until men settled and started to farm, some time after 3000 B.C., that they built themselves more permanent dwellings. They dug circular pits, surrounding them with low banks of earth or stone walls, and into these they embedded branches which met over the middle to form conical or dome-shaped supports for roofs of bracken, turf or skin. In the few places where it was possible to farm and still find enough stones, they used these for the entire shelter, building domes that looked like stone igloos.

By the time the legions of the Emperor Claudius landed in A.D. 43, however, the Britons were living in a variety of dwellings, some of which could almost have been described as houses. The roofs were mostly neat thatch or turf. In the rectangular huts, the branches beneath the roofs rested against a ridge pole which was hung between posts at either end. In the circular huts, they were now supported by posts in the middle, and the walls were much taller and made of thatch or wattle and daub, which was produced by weaving twigs and reeds between close-set vertical stakes, packing them with mud and then leaving it to dry. In a few places, such as Cornwall, there were even some stone-walled buildings which had several rooms set around a courtyard, already imitating the style of the Roman entrepreneurs who had settled in the south after Julius Caesar's expedition in 54 B.C. and had grown rich exporting such commodities as tin, cattle, grain and gold.

In the wake of the legions came governors, bureaucrats, merchants, tradesmen and all the opulent manners and methods of the mightiest empire the world had yet known. The Romans built walled cities, planning them on symmetrical grids and providing them with temples, theatres, public baths and market-places.

Most of the houses had brick walls on the ground floor, with plaster and exposed timbers on the storeys above, foreshadowing the technique which was to become widespread in medieval and Tudor England, and which was to be a favourite with the architects of Victorian and twentieth-century suburbs. Their rooms and corridors opened onto an atrium, a central courtyard, which was sometimes roofed over in the same slate as the rest of the building. They had drains and running water. There were windows in the walls; and there was glass in the windows. Even the smallest houses were heated. The floor of the rooms at ground level was supported on brick piers, and the hot-air passages between these led through holes in the wall to a furnace, which was usually situated beneath the bathroom.

The richest residents of Roman cities were expected to pay for all the public amenities. As a result, many rich men considered it prudent not to live in the cities. Instead they built huge villas on their farms, and the largest of these, which had dozens of rooms and were decorated with stone-faced colonnades, statues and magnificent frescoes and mosaics, were the first great country houses in England.

But the Romans withdrew from the province of Britain at the beginning of the fifth century, and for the next six hundred years it was subjected to a series of invasions, first by Angles, Saxons and Jutes, and later by Vikings from Denmark and Norway. The Roman towns and cities were razed to become the foundations of new settlements. The villas were pillaged and ignored: there is no evidence that a single Saxon ever lived in a Roman villa. All that remains of them to be seen today are their foundations, mosaics and heating systems, such as those at Chedworth and Winchcombe in Gloucestershire, Bignor in Sussex and North Leigh in Oxfordshire.

The Anglo-Saxon kingdoms which emerged eventually

from these invasions blossomed into a great civilisation. Their legal system remains the basis of the laws in Great Britain, the United States and most of the countries in the British Commonwealth. They had a vigorous literature. The style of their illuminated manuscripts is one of the most original and attractive in the whole range of medieval art. Their jewellery and needlework were delicate and complex. They converted to Christianity and built beautiful churches, sometimes using stone from Roman ruins, and occasionally even some of the brick. But very little of this creative energy was devoted to their domestic architecture. The average Saxon villager lived in a hut that was almost identical to his prehistoric predecessor's. If his village was not large enough to have its own church, the only substantial building in it would have been the home of his thegn, the Saxon lord.

The thegn lived in a long hall which was divided internally into quarters for his family, his servants, his farm labourers and even his livestock. It was constructed in a series of bays separated by pairs of huge curved tree-trunks, known as crucks, which were embedded in the ground about sixteen feet apart and met at the top to form the support for a heavy ridge pole. Other timbers, or rafters, were fixed between them, and these, together with the ridge pole, supported a covering of thatch or shingled wood. Only the end walls were vertical, and since the side walls and the roof were in one curved piece, it was only possible to stand upright in the middle. Despite their simple structure, however, the life inside these barn-like buildings was by no means as grim as might be supposed. They were often painted. The internal timbers were richly carved, although it must have been difficult to see the decorations when the fire was lit in the centre of the hall and the smoke was eddying around them searching for the slats in the roof above. And they were the scenes of constant feasting and entertainment. The Saxon thegns were famous for their hospitality; they dined four times a day and drank mead and ale copiously. The Norman chronicler, William of Malmesbury, was not impressed by their domestic habits: 'The custom of drinking together was universal, the night as well as the day being passed in this pursuit. They spent great sums on it while living in small and contemptible houses, unlike the French and Normans, who live at a moderate rate in large and splendid buildings.'

The only surviving examples of these halls are in the European countries where the design originated. On 14 October 1066, the long-haired, ale-swilling Saxons were defeated at Hastings by the short-haired, wine-sipping Nor-

1. Rochester Castle, Kent, the keep, *c.* 1130. Together with Castle Hedingham in Essex, Rochester was one of the first Norman castles in England to be built in stone during the twelfth century. Apart from St Leonard's Tower in Kent and the White Tower at the Tower of London, which were both built by Bishop Gundulph around 1070 and 1080, the earlier Norman castles had been built in timber. The ultimate defensive building, standing within the inner bailey or courtyard, the keep usually contained the great hall, which was the centre of everyday life in the castle. Unlike Castle Hedingham, Rochester still has all its corner towers and embattled parapet, although the windows have been mutilated.

mans. Many of the English halls were destroyed in the campaigns of subjugation that followed, and the others, abandoned by dispossessed thegns, have rotted away with time. But the new rulers created a state so powerful that it was never to be conquered again, and a society so comparatively stable that men began to build their houses in more durable materials. From all the periods that followed, at least some examples have survived.

The Norman king, William the Conqueror, rewarded his followers and the Church which had supported him by granting them estates in England. The new barons and bishops were suddenly immensely rich, and they manifested their great wealth in the magnificence of their stone cathedrals, churches and monasteries. Using the Romanesque style, which, as its name implies, had grown out of the traditions of Rome, they built on a scale that was unrivalled among their contemporaries. The only Saxon churches to survive their energies were in a few rural parishes. Within less than a hundred years, almost every cathedral and abbey in England had been rebuilt.

The barons also built in stone for themselves, erecting tall, sombre castles to replace the wooden ones which had been thrown up hurriedly as soon as possible after the conquest. The central building of the castle was the keep, which was usually rectangular and had walls that were up to twenty feet thick at the base. It could hardly be described as a house, but it had many of the features that were soon to be found in houses as well.

The ground floor was used as a storehouse, the first as quarters for the garrison and servants, and the second, high enough above any assailants to be lit by windows rather than slits, was the great hall, with little bedchambers leading off a gallery above it. The walls of this great hall were plastered and painted with patterns or simple murals; it was often over thirty feet in height and width and as much as forty feet in length; and since the forests of England could not produce roofing beams that were more than twenty feet long, an arch was built across the centre to support them and decorated with zigzag chevron patterns. This was the room where the lord and his family lived and entertained their guests, listening to the songs of their minstrel and dining on food that could seldom have been hot, since it was cooked in another part of the castle to protect the keep from the regular fires that were caused by falling fat from the spits.

The hall was still heated by fires, however, although they were no longer lit on a central hearth. It was the Normans who introduced fireplaces into England. They had no chimneys as yet, the smoke simply drifted out through a flue, and the first of them were no more than recessed openings in the wall surrounded by Romanesque arches and columns. But it was not long before fireplaces became prominent decorative features, with hoods like buttresses over the top and more elaborate columns beneath them. It sometimes took as many as three to heat a great hall effectively: the windows had no glass in them, and when the shutters were opened to let in the light, the cold wind came in as well.

On the rare occasions when the Normans bathed, they used large wooden tubs. But they did have other washing facilities. Near the entrance to the hall there was a basin, known as a laver, where they washed their hands, sometimes to remove the grime before eating with their fingers, and always afterwards to remove the grease.

The rest of the plumbing was rudimentary. The lavatories, or garderobes, with cold stone scats, were built into the thickness of the walls. A few of them had shafts beneath, and there is some evidence that they were flushed by rainwater from the roof, but most of them simply protruded from the keep, allowing the excrement of the household to fall down the outside of the walls, at best into a cesspit, or else into a stagnant moat or a river.

The word garderobe is now the most generally used architectural term for describing these primitive facilities. In fact, however, it is the French for wardrobe, which in the Middle Ages was a small room for storing clothes rather than a piece of furniture, and it was only introduced into England at the beginning of the thirteenth century, when it was regarded as a more polite term than latrine, which itself only means a place in which to wash. Neither word bore any more relation to what actually went on there than the modern terms 'lavatory' and 'toilet'. But civilised societies have always preferred euphemisms for 'the smallest room in the house'. To be fair to them, the medieval English usually referred to it as the 'privy', or privy chamber, which, although still a euphemism, is at least a little less misleading.

2. The great chamber at Castle Hedingham, *c.* 1130. In the best preserved of Norman keeps, this great room is 39 × 31 × 26 feet high. It was built above the inferior or entrance hall, which was itself above a storage chamber. The upper tier of Romanesque arches has simple mouldings like those of the unusually large arch which spans the entire width of the keep. The lower arches and that of the fireplace have added decoration in the form of the chevron pattern cut with either chisel or axe into the moulding. There were two garderobes in this keep, one of which opens off this room.

3. The Manor House, Boothby Pagnell, Lincolnshire, c. 1180. The earliest surviving manor house. The vaulted ground floor was used for storage and the hall or main room could only be reached by the external stair. The kitchen was in a separate wooden building. The stairs, roof and large window are all of a later date.

In the towns around the castles and in the rest of the countryside nearly all the houses were still made out of timber, wattle and daub or cob, which was then just a mixture of mud and straw or gravel. Stone was a very expensive material. Only the cathedrals and castles could justify the cost of transporting it. But in the areas where it was quarried, it was used by a few of the knights for their fortified manor houses and by the richest residents for their houses in the towns.

There were originally only two rooms in the fortified manor houses. The ground floor, which usually had a stone vaulted ceiling, was used, like that of the keep, as a storehouse for the extensive supplies that were required to feed the household throughout the winter. The first floor, which was built at a defensible height and reached by an external staircase, was the hall where the knight and his family lived and slept. It had some of the amenities of the great hall in the castle: there was a fireplace in the middle of the wall, there was often a garderobe and occasionally a laver. The plastered walls were sometimes painted. But the space and the furniture were more limited. At the table, on trestles, where the Normans dined only once a day, the knight sat in the only chair with his family around him on benches.

There are several surviving examples of these fortified manor houses, such as at Boothby Pagnell in Lincolnshire and at Christchurch Castle in Hampshire. But they did not stand as they do today in picturesque isolation. Unlike the castle keeps, they did not have the space to house retainers; they were surrounded by little timber-framed huts and houses; and their kitchens, which were also outside, were often little more than wooden lean-tos built against their stone walls. It was in these ramshackle cook-houses that the Saxon servants roasted oxen and sheep and, wrapping their tongues around the French language, learned to call their cooked meat beef and mutton when they carried it to their Norman master's table.

When King William had conquered England, he introduced a landed hierarchy that was modelled on the feudalism of France. In principle, all land belonged to the king. In return for their great estates, the barons were required to provide him with varying quotas of knights for up to forty days in each year. The barons then sub-let manors in return for the same military service; and on each manor the knight had Saxon tenants, who paid him a proportion of their produce, and serfs, who laboured in his fields and were so much regarded as his property that he could even sell them to pay his debts. But this rigid social structure was not imposed on the market towns. Under the stability of Norman rule, a new merchant class emerged; and some of the stone houses in the towns were built by the most successful of these merchants.

The merchants built in stone to protect their wares against thieves and particularly fires, which were frequent and often devastating among close-set, timber-framed buildings. Their houses were also on two floors, but they had internal staircases. The ground floor was used for storage and business, and like the knights the merchant lived with his family in a first-floor room 'above the shop'. Unfortunately very few examples have survived, but the remains of a house in Southampton, which is known as King John's House, show that the merchants were prepared to spend a great deal of money on them, even if the skill of their masons was not up to the standard of those who worked on the cathedrals and monasteries. It has a fireplace as fine as in many a castle, with a corbled buttress and two carved columns.

This house was built around 1150, sixteen years before King John was born, but there is no evidence that he had anything to do with it. It is simply the earliest of several with which his name is now associated. After a few centuries, men forgot that the merchants of this period had built in stone, and a superstitious tradition arose ascribing structures of unknown origin to some outstandingly evil creator, in particular bad King John and the Devil. For some reason King John got all the houses and the Devil got all the earthworks, such as dykes.

The other stone houses in the towns were built by Jews. Since the Norman barons and clergy did not have the capital to

4. The Jew's House, Lincoln, *c*. 1150. Now much altered, with larger windows inserted and re-roofed, it still has its original Norman arches to the doorway and the two windows on the first floor. These windows would have been of the two-light type like the one at Boothby Pagnell. There was one fireplace above the entrance arch where the now truncated chimney stack can be seen projecting from the surface of the wall.

provide for the building of their castles and cathedrals, they borrowed against the incomes from their rich estates; and since northern Christendom still regarded usury as a sin, they borrowed from the Jews whom William the Conqueror had brought over from Normandy – at an interest of at least 40 per cent. When Aaron of Lincoln, the most famous of these Jews, died in 1185, the debtors on his books included the king of Scotland, five earls, two bishops, an archbishop, nine Cistercian abbeys and the towns of Winchester and Southampton.

The Jews were accustomed to a much higher standard of living than their new neighbours in the English towns. Although their houses were similar to the merchants', they were sometimes partitioned into two or three rooms on each floor, they were more richly decorated, and they were probably better furnished too. But the Jews did not build in stone simply because they could afford to do so. Their houses were also the banks where they kept their gold and silver coins and all the deeds recording their transactions. They had as much to fear from fire and theft as the merchants, and they occasionally had to contend with resentful mobs which tried to break in and destroy their records.

Several of these Jews' houses have survived with very little alteration. Aaron's in Lincoln is no longer standing, but there are three other fine examples in the city, one of which has been

5. Little Wenham Hall, Suffolk, *c.* 1270. A fortified knight's house, this is the earliest surviving brick house in England. The walls of the vaulted storage rooms on the ground floor are four feet thick. The hall on the first floor was accessible from an outside stair as well as internally from the circular staircase in the tower in the angle of the building. This staircase also gives access to the chamber on the top floor and the roof. A small vaulted chapel opens off the hall, which is forty feet long. The Early English Gothic windows with their pointed arches have remained substantially unaltered since the thirteenth century. The bricks vary in size and colour, and the buttresses are all in stone.

wrongly attributed to him. They are solid-looking buildings and surprisingly small, with Romanesque columns and arches around their doorways and windows, sheltering on the steep slope of the hill in the shadow of the massive Christian cathedral.

In the centre of the towns there was not much room for the merchants and Jews to expand their houses. But there was in the country; and it was not long before the knights developed a desire for a little more privacy in their homes. At first they created a separate chamber, which was a sort of private bed-sitting-room, by partitioning one end of their hall with a leather curtain or a wooden screen. By the end of the twelfth century, however, they were extending their houses by building on additional storage space with a great chamber, or solar, above it, such as the one at Boothby Pagnell. The new houses included solars in their original design, and after a while they included chapels as well. One of the loveliest examples of these is Little Wenham Hall in Suffolk, which is also the earliest example of medieval brickwork – so rare that the bricks may well have been imported from Flanders. The solar here was built on a third storey above the chapel, with a spiral staircase leading up to it and out onto the leaded roof of the hall, but in most houses they were on the same level.

Slowly, the manor houses grew. They were still very primitive buildings by the standards of the Roman villas, but they were a new beginning.

CHAPTER 2

Medieval Dwellings

AFTER a particularly severe fire in 1189, during the reign of King Richard the Lionheart, the City of London issued building regulations, offering privileges to those citizens who built stone houses covered with tiles, and ruling that all adjoining houses, whatever else they were made of, should have stone party walls which were to be at least three feet thick and sixteen feet high.

Despite these rules and concessions, however, the majority of London houses during the Middle Ages, like the houses in other towns and cities, had upper storeys which were made out of timber box frames with the panels in between filled with wattle and daub and then covered over with plaster. Until the fourteenth century the roofs were more often thatch than tile, and their only fireproofing was a coat of paint. Although there was plenty of room at the rear of the houses for the gardens where the occupants built their kitchens, grew vegetables and sometimes raised livestock, street frontage was at a premium in the commercial centres; and in other areas most men built as cheaply as possible. As a result, nearly all the houses that were built in rows had their longest walls as party walls and only their gable ends facing the street. The need to save space or materials was always more important than the fear of fire.

For most of the thirteenth century these houses were still very small. Only those that were purely residential had two rooms, with a hall on the ground floor instead of a shop. But by the fourteenth century the box frames had become strong enough to support several storeys. Jetties, or overhangs, were being built, in which huge timbers were used as joists and projected several feet over the street, making the first floor larger than the ground floor; and when a similar jetty was built above, the second floor was even larger still.

The style of the box frames varied: in the east of the country the vertical posts were set close together, with horizontal beams below the windows and at the level of the floors; in the west they were set further apart, with horizontal braces between them, dividing the façade into squares. Either way, there were so many beams and supports that the houses were literally 'half-timbered'. Fires were as frequent and devastating as ever. Many houses were rebuilt several times, and most of the early examples which survived into the age of the

Tudors were rebuilt soon afterwards. There are two fourteenth-century jettied houses still standing in York, but the medieval houses that can be seen today in towns like Canterbury, Shrewsbury and Gloucester were all built towards the end of the fifteenth century.

The life in these town houses was scarcely hygienic. The City of London's building regulations had stipulated that a garderobe pit should be more than three feet from a neighbour's boundary, but this was almost totally ignored, and in London, as in all the other towns, most of the houses that boasted garderobes had them at the front, projecting over the narrow street. Although many towns had public garderobes with cesspits beneath, the citizens who did not live near them and had no such facilities of their own followed the

6. Cottages at Lavenham, Suffolk, *c.* 1490. The overhanging upper storey or jetty was probably first used in the thirteenth century, but by the fifteenth and sixteenth centuries it was a common feature. In the seventeenth century it was outlawed in towns and only used infrequently in the country because of the scarcity of timber. During the seventeenth century many timber-framed buildings were completely plastered over for weather protection.

example of their betters and, rather than pollute their gardens, chucked the contents of whatever receptacle they used as a chamber pot into the street beside the products of the garderobes. And there it all lay for a week or more with the straw that had been used as paper and the rest of the rotting domestic refuse, until a local farmer came to collect it. Cats and dogs and careless people carried it into the houses on their paws and shoes. Disease was rife and plagues were frequent. It was not until 1388 that a parliament sitting in Cambridge passed the first urban sanitation laws. But the efforts to enforce such laws and the attempts to build proper drains never kept up with the rising urban population. Conditions grew worse rather than better, and the burial grounds became so crowded that they sometimes polluted the water supplies.

Nevertheless, there were many ways in which life in even the meanest town house was more comfortable than anywhere other than in a manor house or a castle. Although the house had no oven, it was close to a bakery; although it had no bathroom, it was close to a bath-house. Most of the self-employed tradesmen rented or owned their own little houses, and the many residents of the towns who worked for the merchants, as servants, craftsmen or apprentices, lived with them, like retainers in a castle, sleeping and eating with their families in the chamber or chambers above the shop.

The wealth of the English merchants was founded on the wool trade. After a while they made the natural progression into cloth, and after 1290, when Edward I expelled the Jews, a few of them turned to banking. By the beginning of the fifteenth century they had expanded into many other trades. The richest Lord Mayor of London at that time, Dick Whittington, made his great fortune importing coal from Tyneside in a type of cargo boat known as a cat. With their wealth, their guilds and their self-governing corporations, the leading merchants became as powerful as barons. Many of them still preferred to remain in the commercial centres or market-places, extending their houses at the rear, building on jetties and additional storeys and embellishing the timbers with elaborate carving. But there were some who moved out to the less crowded parts of the towns, where there were open spaces and even farms, and built themselves free-standing houses, often in stone, which were like the manor houses in the country. And there were even quite a few merchants who aspired to join the ranks of the gentry and bought country estates and built manor houses there. Many of the great county families of western England were founded by merchants: one of them, William Grevel, built a stone house in 1400 which

142,143

7. Grevel House, Chipping Campden, *c.* 1400. This wool merchant's house in a prosperous town in the Cotswolds still has its bay window – one of the earliest existing examples. Apart from the beautifully carved mouldings and the Gothic details of this window, the plain surfaces have been carefully cut and laid, in marked contrast to the much rougher stonework of the walls on either side.

still stands in Chipping Campden in Gloucestershire, now one of the prettiest villages in England but then a busy collecting centre for the wool trade. And in Kent, in 1341, Sir John de Poultney, who was four times Lord Mayor of London, built the manor house which remains the core of one of the finest medieval houses in England, Penshurst Place.

Although the towns grew larger during the Middle Ages, the vast majority of the population lived and worked in the countryside. During the thirteenth century most families were still living in smoke-filled huts without even a window or a vent in the thatch. The rushes on the damp earth floors were changed so seldom that they rotted, and they were thick with the droppings of a few chickens and perhaps a pig, or two or three precious sheep in winter time.

It was not until the fourteenth century that a few villagers began to build cruck cottages. These were built on the same principle as a single bay in a Saxon hall, with timber frames on stone plinths, but they had much more headroom now: the edges of the thatched roofs were supported by a beam that rested on a row of upright posts in the wattle and daub walls

26

beyond the base of the crucks. The conditions inside were little better than in the huts. The floors were still rush-covered earth. The furniture was never more than a few stools and a board on trestles or tree-trunks for a table. When the family needed bowls and spoons to eat with, they had to carve them out of wood themselves, and the beds, where they slept fully clothed and often without a blanket to cover them, were only bags of straw or heather.

The fortunes of villages fluctuated. Bad harvests brought famine. The rise in population meant that many men had enough sons to fulfil their feudal duties as well as till their own smallholdings, but for the serfs, whose plots were tiny, it also increased the number of mouths that those plots had to feed. Nevertheless, there were some areas where the villages grew progressively more prosperous. The peasants who grazed sheep on common land were the largest suppliers of the wool market. Some of them earned enough to set themselves up as yeoman farmers, and many built box-framed cottages with two rooms in them, a houseplace and a bower, although in most cases their families lived only in the bower and used the houseplace as a cattle shed.

As the use of money became more widespread, landlords preferred to collect rents in cash rather than in field service and to pay cash wages, even to their serfs. As a result, some serfs were able to buy their freedom and build better homes for their families. Gradually, the number of cottages increased.

After the Black Death had reduced the population of England from about four million in 1348 to about two and a half million in 1349, many villagers migrated illegally to take advantage of the opportunities in the half-empty towns. Free labourers charged such high wages that they had to be limited by statute, and the landlords reverted to field service, imposing intolerable burdens on their surviving serfs and tenants. But the plague and the migrations had left empty cottages into which more serfs could move their families, and without men to work it, land was cheap. Some peasant farmers rented tracts so large that they were able to buy more with the income, raising their sons to the ranks of the yeomanry and their grandsons to the ranks of the gentry. One such was Clement Paston of Norfolk, who earned enough to educate his son as a lawyer. Within two generations the family owned many manors, and the letters which it has left to posterity are an invaluable and enchanting insight into the life in medieval manor houses.

The cottages of the peasantry and yeomanry were rebuilt by almost every generation that lived in them, and this process, together with the same building techniques, continued into the reign of the Tudors. It is unlikely that there are any cottages in England today that were built before the sixteenth century. But there are many Tudor examples which have incorporated these buildings or show what their frames must have looked like, and there is even a cruck cottage at Didbrook in Gloucestershire which was built around 1520.

The greatest advances in domestic architecture and living standards during the Middle Ages took place inevitably in the houses of the rich landed families. At the beginning of the thirteenth century, all the houses were fortified. Like Little Wenham or Old Soar in Kent, their halls were on the first floor, and the house and the courtyard of farm buildings in front of it were surrounded by a wall and usually a moat with a drawbridge and a gatehouse. But by the end of that century, half the new houses had been built with their halls on the ground floor. Their owners regarded it as enough to have a defensive wall and a moat. As the need for defence continued to decline, the ground-floor hall became the norm, and by the beginning of the fifteenth century the only fully fortified houses were being built in the really dangerous areas, like the borders of Scotland.

9. (*Right*) Hull Manor House, Yorkshire, 1542–3. This drawing was made when the considerable additions to the house had just been finished. The medieval gateway to the right-hand courtyard is clearly shown with its Gothic windows. The great hall forms the division between the two courtyards in a position that occurs in the plans of other houses, notably Haddon Hall. The building that has been added to it on the right may well have been new apartments for its owner. The other ranges that surround the courtyards would almost certainly have been lodgings for guests and upper servants. The building in the foreground, with a two-light Gothic window high up in its walls, would have been the kitchen.

8. Cottage at Didbrook, Gloucestershire, *c.* 1520. The pair of inclined crucks are clearly visible in the gable-end wall. Originally the roof would have followed these main structural timbers almost to the ground. This very primitive form of construction had the serious disadvantage of restricted headroom and it was for this reason that corner posts and other structural timbers were superimposed to gain height inside the cottage. The crucks rested on a horizontal beam raised above the earth on stones.

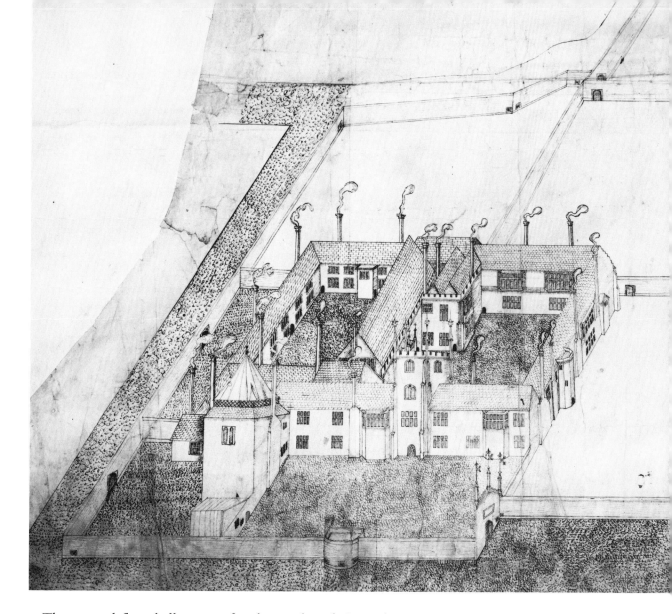

The ground-floor halls were often larger than their predecessors. Before the beginning of the fourteenth century, when the English carpenters developed the systems of beams and rafters for which they were to become acknowledged masters, most of the halls were aisled, with rows of columns down either side supporting the heavy beams above. They were also taller than they had been, and since this made them more difficult to heat, their owners reverted to a hearth in the centre of a floor that was now no more than packed earth. The beams were high enough to be clear of sparks, and the smoke escaped through louvres, like large lanterns on top of the roof with pottery sides with holes in them, or else wooden slats which could be opened and shut by cords in the hall.

Initially, most manor houses followed an L-shaped plan and were made out of whichever of the two principal materials was most readily available: timber frames in the east and south and stone along the limestone belt that crosses England through the Cotswolds from Portland Bill to Lincolnshire. In the corner of the house where the cross-wing joined the hall there was a little tower containing the internal staircase that led up to the solar and the chapel; and below these, where there had once been a storeroom, there was a pantry where the bread was kept and a buttery for the wine and beer, each with its own door into the hall. The kitchen was still a separate building and the food was carried from it across a covered walkway and into the hall through a passage between the pantry and the buttery. But by now the kitchen was much more substantial: it was often stone vaulted with a louvre in the roof, or, like the one at Stanton Harcourt in Oxfordshire, had a timber roof with slats in each bay.

At the opposite, or upper, end of the hall, the lord of the manor and his guests and family sat at a high table which was raised on a dais and lit by a Gothic window in the wall above. In winter, each time a service door opened at the lower end it created a draught which chilled the hall and shrouded him in a gust of smoke from the central fire. But after a while movable wooden screens were made which could be placed in front of the doors during dinner. None of the earliest of these has survived, although there is a late one, carved at the end of the fifteenth century, at Rufford Old Hall in Lancashire.

The arrangement of the hall also meant that when the lord had dined he had to step down from the dais and make his way through his retainers and their food scraps on the floor to reach his own private chamber. As a result, when the manor houses became larger at the end of the thirteenth century, the new rooms were added in a second wing which was built at the upper end of the hall, and thereafter the H-plan which this created became one of the standard patterns for medieval manor houses.

Behind the high table there was now a storeroom, which later developed into a parlour, with a chapel beside it under a separate roof; and at the side there was a bay containing the staircase that led up to the solar, or great chamber. This left a spare chamber at the lower end above the buttery and pantry, which could be used for guests, or the son and heir, or the most important retainer, the steward, who managed the estate; and when the storeroom became a parlour this, too, could be used for guests, although for the most distinguished visitors the lord of the manor often gave up his solar.

10. Rufford Old Hall, Lancashire, c. 1500. The great hall has a free-standing screen dividing the main body of the hall from the screen's passage. The doorways to the pantry and buttery behind the screen have been blocked up. The moveable screen is extremely rare. Its three finials are later additions. Decoration has run riot in this comparatively small hall, and the considerable complexity and amount of woodwork used bears little relationship to the structural requirements. The hammer-beam roof, for example, is rare in a room of this size.

The private chambers had fireplaces, and during the fourteenth century they acquired chimneys, which rose above the roof and became more and more elaborate as time went on. Like the hall, the private chambers had thick wooden shutters that closed over iron bars in the glassless windows. Their floors were mostly strewn with rushes and their furniture was still sparse, consisting of little more than a heavy chair, chests, benches and a bed. But in many of the more prosperous houses the lower parts of the walls were covered with simple wooden panelling, or wainscoting. Some had warm woollen hangings decorated with religious or heraldic scenes, and in a few houses there was the occasional precious rug, brought back from the Middle East by a crusader or a merchant.

Whether they had panelling or not, however, the walls were nearly always brightly painted. When the sheriff of Wiltshire received orders concerning alterations to King Henry III's house at Clarendon, he was instructed 'to wainscot the king's lower chamber, and to paint that wainscot a green colour, and to put a border to it, and to cause the heads of kings and queens to be painted on the borders; and to paint on the walls of the king's upper chamber the story of Saint Margaret Virgin, and the four Evangelists; and to paint the wainscot of the same chamber of a green colour spotted with gold, and to paint on it heads of men and women; and all these paintings are to be done with good and exquisite colours.'

At the same time as the H-plan was evolving, tower houses were also being built. In some of these the tower contained all the rooms, which led to a revival of the first-floor hall, but in many the tower was built at one end of the hall over the solar, which, with the little Gothic windows, made them look more like churches than houses. With the defiant air of a castle keep, the tower was intended to reflect the prestige of its occupant, and many of these houses were built by men who were not descended from landed families. One of the most interesting, Longthorpe Tower in Cambridgeshire, was built around 1300 by Robert Thorpe, who was the great-grandson of a serf and served at Peterborough Abbey as steward.

This house is outstanding not only because it is a fine example of the combination of tower and hall but also because in 1945, when it was evacuated by the Home Guard, wall paintings were found beneath the whitewash and distemper which have been described as 'by far the most impressive piece of medieval secular mural decoration in the country'. They include astonishingly delicate scenes of the nativity, the seven ages of man, the labours of the month, the Wheel of Five Senses, birds, animals and the figure of a king, who is either

Edward II or Edward III. The work bears a remarkable similarity to the Peterborough Psalter, which was finished in 1321; and the king's coat of arms is represented by three leopards, without the fleurs-de-lis of France, which were added by Edward III in 1340. From this it seems likely that it was carried out between these years and was commissioned by Robert's son, who was also steward at Peterborough Abbey, or perhaps by one of his distinguished grandsons, either Sir Robert, who rose to be Edward III's Chancellor, or Sir William, who became Lord Chief Justice of England.

Towards the end of the fourteenth century some houses became larger still when parts of their courtyards were turned into lodgings for guests and senior retainers. By then a great lord could have as many as 150 men in his household, and they did not all come from humble stock like his scullions and porters. The steward, the chamberlain, who ran the house, the treasurer, the keeper of the wardrobe, the knights, and in large households many others like the yeoman of the pantry and the

11. Longthorpe Tower, Cambridgeshire, c. 1300. The unique wall paintings in the great chamber of the Tower at Longthorpe, only discovered in 1945, are an indication of one type of decoration used in medieval houses. Since Longthorpe was neither a great house nor the home of some important personage, it must be assumed that a number of houses were originally decorated in this way.

buttery, all came from landed families. Barons were served by gentlemen, and in their own houses gentlemen were served by lesser gentlemen or yeomen. It was considered an honour to wear the livery of a great man, and serving in his household was one of the ways in which younger sons could earn enough to buy land and build manor houses of their own.

The youngest servants in the household, the pages, who were there as much to learn as to serve, came from families which were the social equals of their masters'. The English upper classes have almost always sent their sons to be educated away from home. Even the Saxons did it. There was only a period of a few generations after the end of the Middle Ages when they educated them at home with tutors before they began to send them away again to school. In the great houses, which Ben Johnson later described as 'noble nurseries', young men who might one day own such houses themselves were taught how to run them and how to ride and fight. They studied under a grammar master, they learned courtly manners and, in waiting on the lord's every whim at table or in his private chambers, they learned a little temporary humility. The heirs to dukedoms who served as pages in medieval households could be subjected to as much domestic indignity as their descendants were to suffer as fags at Eton during the eighteenth and early nineteenth centuries.

At first only senior retainers, such as the steward and the chamberlain, had lodgings of their own. There was only one knight's chamber, and where there was no boy's chamber the pages slept with the other body servants outside their master's door. Lesser servants slept round the fires in the hall or the kitchen, and the few women in the household, such as nurses or women of the lady's chamber, had no more privacy than the knights. The hall was still the centre of their lives. It was there, as always, that the lord held his manorial court. It was there that he received guests, gave banquets and watched the entertainments of travelling jugglers, tumblers and players. And it was there that the entire household assembled each day before noon to dine and again to sup in the early evening.

Few lords had platters and goblets that were made out of anything better than pewter, and even these were shared between two people. Such gold and silver as they had was only used for decoration. There were never enough knives and spoons at high tables and most guests brought their own. The meat was eaten off flat loaves, known as trenchers, which soaked up the sauces and the fat and were then thrown to the hounds or carried across to the gatehouse and given to the poor. But the hospitality at high tables was prodigious. The

12. The courtyard at Haddon Hall, Derbyshire, 1300–30. The exterior of the central core of a medieval house contained the great hall in the centre, the pantry and buttery to the left and the owner's apartments on the right of the hall. The plan of this section of Haddon is remarkably similar to that of Penshurst Place. With minor variations it was the plan adopted for both great houses and small manors and even yeomen's farmhouses. It remained a standard plan even during much of Queen Elizabeth's reign. Unlike Penshurst, Haddon had a fireplace in the wall of the great hall, the chimney stack being castellated, like the hall itself, the porch and the pantry and buttery. The first floor of the upper or owner's end of the building was the solar – the bed-sitting-room of the owner – below which was the parlour. Above the pantry and buttery were further chambers for guests.

surviving menus of some medieval banquets include such adventurous dishes as the flesh of whale, seal and bear. There were three meats at almost every meal. Sauces were rich and highly spiced, fruit was imported at great expense, and the confectioners composed exotic sweetmeats which were carved to represent heraldic or legendary scenes. In the century when the English language replaced French at the tables of the aristocracy, the Anglo-Saxon social attitudes ousted the Norman moderation. The late-fourteenth-century lord of the manor was expected to live lavishly, and many of them did so far beyond their means.

There was one way, however, in which Franco-Norman attitudes dominated. Everything was accompanied by meticulous ceremony, including the laying of the table. The arrival of each course was heralded by pipes, trumpets and tabours. Pages served their masters on bended knee and bowed each time they were spoken to. Even washing before the meal had become part of the ceremony: guests were given bowls and napkins on arrival or else waited for their turn at the lavers, which were now filled from decorated cisterns made out of lead or stone. One of these, made as early as 1330, has survived at Battle Hall in Kent and is shaped like the twin towers of a castle with a lion's head as a spout.

At the beginning of the fifteenth century the movable screens at the lower end of the hall began to be replaced by permanent screens that ran across its full width and had three doors in them which were not opened until the service doors beyond them had been closed. Like the beams and rafters, they were heavily carved, and the area above them was soon floored over and turned into a gallery for the minstrels.

And yet at this very moment when the halls had reached the height of their splendour, the lords of the manors decided that it was no longer seemly to eat in company with their servants. Instead they withdrew to dine with their guests in the parlour or beneath the oriel window of the great chamber above it. The new custom had begun among kings and dukes in the middle of the fourteenth century and had worked its way downwards through society until, by the middle of the fifteenth century, in all but the smallest manor houses the hall had been left to retainers and servants. It was a division that was to survive, like the word hall itself, for so long as there were servants in houses. Even during the twentieth century the people who served at the tables of dining-rooms ate their own meals in a servants' hall.

13. The great hall, Penshurst Place, Kent, *c*. 1340. Joseph Nash's nineteenth-century view of feasting in the great hall, showing the entrance of the Yule log.

14. The great hall, Penshurst Place. The least altered of medieval halls, 62 feet long and 39 feet wide, Penshurst was built for a rich London merchant. The screen, with its gallery above, was installed in the latter half of the sixteenth century, and beyond can be seen the door to the buttery. Two other doors, hidden by the central part of the screen, led to the kitchen passage and the pantry. The roof construction above this large hall, compared with that of Rufford Old Hall (plate 10), is restrained and functional. The central hearth is unusual in not having been replaced by a fireplace in the wall.

15. Ightam Mote, Kent, c. 1340–1520. This timber and stone house developed round a courtyard and is encircled by a moat. In places, the timber-framed upper storeys are jettied out over the water. With its endless changes of roof-line, its variety of windows and mixture of building materials, it is a perfect example of a picturesque house. This is a view of the earliest part of the building.

There were several who applauded the move. One anonymous fifteenth-century poet wrote:

Pope, Emperor, King Cardinal,
Prince with golden royal rod,
Duke, Archbishop in his pall;
All these for their dignity
Ought not to dine in a hall.

But there were also many who were saddened by it and regretted the loss of that 'Merrie England' which all Englishmen believe existed in an earlier age than their own. When the custom was just beginning, William Langland wrote in *Piers Plowman*:

Wretched is the hall . . . each day in the week
There the Lord and Lady liketh not to sit.
Now have the rich a rule to eat by themselves
In a privy parlour . . . for poor men's sake,
Or in a chamber with a chimney, and leave the chief hall
That was made for meals, for men to eat in.

In some houses the lord and his lady still dined in the hall on great occasions, but in most of the new houses the great chambers were so large that they could accommodate a banquet. In these the two rooms were usually called the upper and lower hall. But there is evidence that in at least one of them they may have been used at different times of year. At the house in Norfolk known as Caister Castle, which was built by Sir John Fastolf, who had fought in France with King Henry V, they were referred to as the summer and winter halls.

16. The interior of one of the upper rooms at Ightam Mote is perhaps less picturesque but typical of many medieval and Tudor rooms in countless houses all over England. In many smaller houses it would have been the grandest room after the great hall.

During the fifteenth century the manor houses became much larger and more splendid. Many more chambers were added to the private apartments for the lord and his family. In some houses a ceiling was built over the hall, which meant that once again it was heated by a fireplace, and the space above was turned into bedchambers or a dormitory for retainers. Kitchens were incorporated into the main body of the building, gatehouses became towers, and more and more lodgings were built until these and the kitchen took up the whole courtyard between the gatehouse and the hall and made the house look like the university colleges from which the idea had evolved. Some new houses incorporated all the chambers they needed in an enlarged H-plan and were built without any wall or courtyard, although they usually had a decorative moat and a gatehouse which stood in splendid isolation. Cothay Manor in Somerset was built to this plan as late as 1480.

17. Cothay Manor, Somerset, c. 1480. A perfect and little-altered example of the central core of houses like Penshurst and Haddon reduced in scale to the extent that here it forms the whole house. The wing to the left is later, and almost certainly built on the site of the former kitchen. The gatehouse, however, is contemporary with the main building and would have provided lodgings for guests. The upper end chambers – the parlour with the solar above – are on the right. Both this upper end and the lower project forward from the central hall as cross wings so that the plan of the house is in the form of an 'H'.

Many of the half-timbered manor houses were now being built with jetties like the town houses. To some extent this may have been a matter of fashion, but there was also a practical reason for it. When the ends of the joists in the upper storey rested on the timbers in the outer wall, the middle of the floor was often disconcertingly springy. When they projected a few feet over them, it was not. It is quite likely that the builders had discovered this by accident after more than a hundred years of experience on town houses, but it is also possible that by now they had learned a few principles of mechanics from their more accomplished colleagues who worked on cathedrals, and had realised that the weight of the upper walls on each end of the joists was actually lifting the load from their centres.

It was again during the fifteenth century that glass, which had long been used in the windows of cathedrals, began to be used in houses as well, in little square or diamond-shaped pieces held together by strips of lead. It was still very expensive and at first it was imported. Small manors could not afford it, and some lords used it only in the tops of their windows, so that there would at least be some light in the chambers when the shutters beneath were closed. But the richest lords went so far as to enlarge their windows and use pieces of stained glass to decorate them with their armorial bearings. One such window, made in 1465 for Sir John Norreys, has survived at Ockwells Manor in Berkshire, which also contains one of the earliest surviving examples of a fixed screen.

Two other important innovations were brought back from France by the men who had fought there during the Hundred Years War. The first of these was the house with more than one courtyard. To some extent this was evolving anyway: in those houses where the single courtyard was entirely taken up by lodgings and kitchens, the stables and other farm buildings were turning into a second courtyard in front of it. But in the French plan the 'inner courtyard' was built at the rear with the hall running across the building between this and what was now the 'outer courtyard'. When these second courtyards were added to such great houses as Penshurst Place or Haddon Hall in Derbyshire, which had been growing steadily since the twelfth century, they almost doubled them in size.

Some of the new houses which were built to this pattern also used the second, and by far the most significant, innovation – a material which had impressed the English with its colour, versatility and practicality. Although they had been baking clay tiles since the end of the thirteenth century, they had no

18. (*Left*) The Old Hall,
Gainsborough, Lincolnshire,
c. 1475. The bay window at the
upper end of the hall was a
refinement in later medieval
houses to shed more light on
the end of the hall where the
owner sat with his guests on a
raised dais. Here the elaborate
vaulting and fine tracery of the
windows is in marked contrast
to the rest of the hall, which is
timber-framed.

19. Oxburgh Hall, Norfolk,
1482. The gatehouse, which
rises from a moat, gives access
to the courtyard across which
lies the great hall. Although
building began here in the last
years of the Wars of the Roses,
the house was built as a 'castle'
for decoration and prestige
rather than defence. The
gatehouse was the only part of
the original medieval house
which was designed to be
symmetrical.

word for this material until they adopted the French one. At last, the English were building in brick.

When he built Caister Castle in brick between 1443 and 1446, Sir John Fastolf gave it as many as three courtyards in a row. The central courtyard was separated from the others by a surrounding moat, which was connected to the River Bure so that Sir John could travel to Yarmouth in his barge, and in its western corner, also following the French tradition, there was a lofty tower with five storeys in it. Even this, however, was not as impressive as the six-storey brick tower which was built at the same time at Tattershall Castle in Lincolnshire by his friend Ralf, Lord Cromwell, who was Lord Chief Treasurer of the Exchequer.

Like many, these men gave their houses battlements and intended that they should look like castles: at the end of the thirteenth century, Edward I had forbidden the building of castles without royal consent, and since then men had acquired the 'licence to crenellate' as evidence of their authority. The houses were hardly formidable defences and they were imposing rather than beautiful, but within forty years there was a brick manor house in Norfolk which was much more harmonious and restrained. In 1482 Sir Edmund Bedingfield built Oxburgh Hall around one huge courtyard with a seven-storey towered gatehouse, and he set it in the middle of a moat so wide that when men rode up they saw the whole house mirrored in it.

The furniture in the mid-fifteenth-century manor houses was still very limited and simple, but the interior decoration was now much more elaborate. Rich men had windows set more than ten feet from the floor to make way for their precious tapestries beneath, and by the end of the century the walls of some principal chambers were completely covered in panelling which was moulded with hollow and rounded planes into a 'linenfold' pattern that represented the falling folds of a table-cloth or a canopy on a bed. The best tapestries of this period were known as Arras, after the town in Artois where they were made, and they depicted the same variety of subjects as the wall paintings they replaced. Some rich men bought them in sets for particular chambers and even had several sets which were hung at different times of year. Sir John Fastolf, for example, had scenes of hunting and hawking for autumn and of shepherds for summer, and apart from these he had pieces of Arras depicting the Siege of Falaise, the Nine Paladins, the Assumption of the Virgin and 'a lady harping by a castle'.

By now all the bedchambers and lodgings in the larger

manor houses were equipped with their own laver and garderobe, and the latter always had a little window which provided useful light as well as necessary ventilation – the fourteenth-century Life of Saint Gregory had recommended it as a place for reading undisturbed.

Bathing had become a much more regular habit: it was regarded as courteous to offer a bath to guests after a journey or to knights after a joust or a hunt. The baths were still wooden tubs, however, covered with canopies and padded with cloth, and the hot water to fill them had to be heated in earthen pots and then bailed out afterwards. But a few of the great houses and the royal palaces had bathrooms with tiled floors and cisterns under which fires could be lit. The first recorded instance of hot and cold running water was as long ago as 1351, when Edward III installed two cisterns for the purpose at Westminster and paid a certain Robert Foundour fifty-six shillings and eight pence for two large bronze taps.

The water supply was often carried to the houses in pipes made of wood and later lead, and drains were built to take away the waste from the lavers and the sinks in the kitchens. But where there was no moat or river the garderobes still discharged their contents down a shaft to a cesspit with an arch built over it in the wall. These had to be emptied by hand, and by the end of the fifteenth century the specialists who performed this service had become known as 'gong fermers'. It was a nasty job, but they were well paid for it. In 1406 one Thomas Watergate received as much as forty shillings 'for cleaning out and cleansing a latrine under the chamber of the keeper of the king's Privy Seal and cleaning out two drains leading from the king's cellar to the Thames'.

By the end of the fifteenth century there were still plenty of hovels in the villages around the manor houses. But besides these there were now cottages and little yeomen's farmhouses. Above all, the manor houses themselves had proliferated. Some had been built by merchants, many by families who had risen from bondage – the Thorpes and the Pastons were by no means unusual – and many had been built by the younger sons of landed families who had saved their salaries in the service of great lords, or who had even earned their fortunes in trade. Unlike their descendants and their European contemporaries, the English gentry had not yet denied themselves the opportunities of commerce by branding it with a snobbish social stigma – Dick Whittington was the youngest son of a knight from Gloucestershire. There were now many more varying degrees of wealth than there had been at the end of the twelfth century, when hovels were home to everyone in the

countryside other than lords and their retainers.

The English house had come a long way in more than three centuries of evolution, from Boothby Pagnell to Oxburgh Hall, and from the little stone houses of the Jews to the imposing timber mansions of the merchants. Nevertheless, there was little in the English countryside that was as splendid as the great new châteaux of France, London was no match for Paris and neither had anything to compare with Venice. The largest manor houses of England had grown up piecemeal over the centuries. With its high walls, towers and irregular rooflines, Haddon Hall looks more like a little fortified town than a house.

After the first half of the fifteenth century the noble families that might have built new houses were preoccupied by the fierce civil war that ended in 1485 with the Battle of Bosworth Field and the accession of Henry Tudor, Earl of Richmond. Some of them were ruined by the war for ever, others took years to recover their fortunes. Meanwhile the new houses were built by the 'New Men' of the Tudor age, who had far too much pride and ambition simply to expand their modest manors. They preferred the example of Sir Edmund Bedingfield. Haddon Hall was a thing of the past: Oxburgh was the shape of things to come.

20. Penshurst Place, Kent. From the air, the house can be seen spreading out in all directions as later sections were added to the central medieval core.

CHAPTER 3

The Tudor Age

T HE event that had the most profound effect on the buildings of the sixteenth century had absolutely nothing to do with architecture. In 1534, Parliament passed the Act of Supremacy recognising King Henry VIII as supreme head of the English Church. England had rejected the authority of Rome. In the years that followed, in a Protestant kingdom, the monasteries were dissolved and the power and privilege of the clergy were reduced.

For architecture the result was twofold. In the first place, the emphasis shifted from ecclesiastical to secular building. The masterpieces of England's medieval architecture are her abbeys and cathedrals. It is hard to believe that the simple stone manor house at Boothby Pagnell was built over forty years after the completion of the magnificent Romanesque cathedral at Durham, or that the hall of Penshurst Place, fine though it is, is exactly contemporary with the breathtaking Gothic choir in the cathedral at Gloucester. But the masterpieces of Tudor architecture are houses. After the Reformation, few churches were begun: the great buildings were erected, not to the glory of God, but for the glorification of the men who lived in them.

In the second place, the break with Rome also meant a break with Catholic Europe, and this in turn meant a loss of contact with the most important centres of contemporary culture. The direct influence of the flourishing Italian Renaissance, which had already taken root in France, had reached England before the Reformation, encouraged by the patronage of Henry VIII. His father's tomb at Westminster Abbey had been sculpted by the Florentine Pietro Torrigiano; Italian craftsmen had come to work on English houses. But after the Reformation that influence was only second-hand, interpreted, often clumsily, from books, or imported in a modified form from Protestant Germany, Holland and Flanders. During the century when the domestic architecture of England received its first great impetus, it was left on its own to evolve as it pleased in a style that was uniquely English. In his *Description of England*, written early in the reign of Queen Elizabeth I, the Reverend William Harrison wrote: 'If ever curious buildings did flourish in England, it is in these our years, wherein our workmen excel.'

21. Compton Wynyates, Warwickshire, c. 1525. Once surrounded by a moat, Compton Wynyates must have been even more romantic than when this photograph was taken. Since then, the magnificent nineteenth-century topiary garden has been uprooted. This was one of the first of many great brick houses built during Henry VIII's reign. It was the Tudors who re-established the brick industry that had disappeared with the Romans. Only a few houses were built of brick before Tudor times, of which Little Wenham was the earliest and Oxburgh the last. Both were built in areas where clay was plentiful, but Compton Wynyates lies in the limestone belt that sweeps across England from Yorkshire to Dorset.

The great Tudor houses that were built before the Reformation were already enormous by the standards of the previous century. Hengrave Hall in Suffolk had forty bedchambers. Like many, it was built by a merchant, but there were many others which were built by Henry VIII's courtiers. Compton Wynyates in Warwickshire, for example, was built by a merchant who became his Esquire of the Body; Layer Marney in Essex was built by the Captain of his Bodyguard; Hampton Court in Middlesex by Cardinal Wolsey, the butcher's son who rose to be his Lord Chancellor; and Sutton Place in Surrey by the Cardinal's assistant, Sir Richard Weston.

These houses had a great deal in common. To start with, they were all brick. In style and design, Compton Wynyates is the natural development of the medieval pattern, and the others, with their crenellations, courtyards and towers, appear at first sight to be the same. The gatehouse at Layer Marney, with magnificent eight-storey towers on either side of it, seems simply to be the latest and largest in the tradition of Tattershall and Oxburgh. But on closer inspection it is much more than that. The first timid symptoms of all the major developments in the design and decoration of sixteenth-century houses are contained in this one gatehouse.

22. Sutton Place, Surrey, *c.* 1525. The decoration over the entrance door of this brick house is, like the surrounds to the door and windows and other decorative details, made of terracotta. It was designed and executed by Italian craftsmen who had been brought to England by Henry VIII. At Sutton the predominantly cream colour of the terracotta contrasts rather unhappily with the red brick.

The battlements are shells with dolphins leaping over them, and like the surrounds to the windows they are made of terracotta. The windows at Sutton Place are similar, and there are twelve cupids on terracotta plaques above the entrance to its hall. At Hengrave, the shield below the window of the gatehouse is supported by terracotta statues of cupids in Roman armour, and at Hampton Court the towers that flank the gatehouse contain terracotta roundels depicting Roman emperors. All these were either made by Italians or copied by Englishmen from Italian models. They are the first examples of Renaissance decoration. At East Barsham Manor in Norfolk, which was built at the same time, the Italian terracotta technique was used to coat the entire house in traditional Gothic decorations, but in the second half of the sixteenth century, after the arrival of Dutch and Flemish masons, the great stone houses were equally coated in decorations which, like the dolphins and cupids, were entirely classical in origin.

23. East Barsham Manor, Norfolk, c. 1525. Smaller than Sutton Place, and much further away from London, East Barsham has none of the Renaissance details that the Italians had used at Sutton. But here the colour of the terracotta decoration matches the colour of the brick – the same clay being used for both – and as a result the effect is much less harsh. The skills of the craftsmen in the use of clay, both in ordinary and moulded bricks, as well as in terracotta, make an early appearance in this delightful, if eccentric, house.

24. Layer Marney Hall, Essex, *c.* 1525. The vast gatehouse was designed as the entrance to a great courtyard house which was never finished. The two chambers on the floors above the entrance arch are flanked by the eight-storeyed towers which contained lodgings for guests. The huge windows that light the two chambers have terracotta mullions and a single cross member or transom, all elaborately decorated with Renaissance detail. As a building, this tower is a positive statement both in its scale and in its symmetry, and like Sutton Place, where the whole entrance front is arranged symmetrically, it represents an early example of a new approach to the design of English houses.

The towers at Layer Marney are also symmetrical in every detail. At Sutton Place the whole house is symmetrical. This, too, is in the manner of the Renaissance. After the middle of the sixteenth century, symmetry was a universal feature of great houses. But to some extent this was due to a fashion for symbolism, a belief that the household was a microcosm of society, and that the order and proportion of the household should be reflected in the house itself. It was in decoration rather than design that the influence of the Renaissance was strongest. The classical form of the Italian house was not yet to replace the Gothic plan, and it was in the fusion of the two styles, Gothic and Renaissance, that the English houses were 'curious' and unique. Apart from their symmetry, and despite their profusion of Classical columns and other ebullient Renaissance decorations, the great English houses at the end of the century were still essentially Gothic in their structure.

There is one other way in which the gatehouse at Layer Marney differs from the earlier towers and foreshadows the style of the houses to come. The window above the entrance is much larger. Even at the end of the previous century the manor houses and 'castles' had all their large windows facing inwards onto their courtyards – the oriel windows on the outside walls of Oxburgh were added during nineteenth-century restorations, and the other manor houses which now have large windows facing outwards only do so because these, too, have been added, or else because their courtyards have gone. But after 1485 the nostalgia for the military past was dying. At the end of the Hundred Years War in France, thousands of professional soldiers had returned to England without any means of earning their living. On the outbreak of the Wars of the Roses, these men had joined either side or both and had fought with an experienced ferocity such as England had not seen since the twelfth century, murdering and pillaging wherever they went. The unsurprising result of this was that when the wars were over the English were left with a profound distaste for soldiers and everything to do with them. For the next 150 years, while the rest of Europe was reorganising and modernising its armies, England made do with its county levies. It was no longer fashionable to affect the style of a soldier. The fashion now was for the airs of a courtier and a scholar. Great houses were built to entertain monarchs. They were ostentatiously open to the world, with windows that reflected the wealth of the owner and classical decorations that reflected his learning. Long before the end of the sixteenth century, when Hardwick Hall was said to be more glass than wall, the great houses of England were all defiantly indefensible.

Appropriately, the last of the old-style 'castles', Thornbury in Gloucestershire, was begun in 1511 by the great Edward de Stafford, Duke of Buckingham, the most senior among the remnants of the feudal nobility with the same royal blood in his veins as the Tudors. But the house, like the proud duke, was already an anachronism; and he never lived to see it finished. One day, while waiting on Henry VIII at dinner, he was holding a bowl in which the king had washed his hands, when Cardinal Wolsey, who sat next to the king, presumed to dip his hands in it too. Irritated by the impertinent disparagement of his rank, the duke spilled the contents on the cardinal's shoes. Wolsey swore vengeance. With the help of a steward whom Buckingham had dismissed for oppressing his tenants, he trumped up a charge of treason, claiming that the duke had designs on the throne. Convicted on the evidence of the steward, the duke refused to plead for his sovereign's mercy, and on 17 May 1521 he was executed. When the news reached Europe, the Emperor Charles V was heard to exclaim: 'A butcher's dog has killed the finest buck in England.'

The fashion for 'castles' died with the duke. But by then the fashion for the huge houses which the architectural historian Sir John Summerson described as 'prodigious' was already well under way. Henry VII had started the fashion for 'prodigy houses' when he made up for the paucity and modesty of royal residences by building an enormous new palace at Richmond in Surrey, which was completed in 1501. His son, Henry VIII, continued in the royal tradition: in 1538 he razed the Surrey village of Ewell to build the fantastic Nonesuch Palace. Neither of these palaces has survived: Richmond was knocked down by Oliver Cromwell and Nonesuch was given by Charles II to one of his mistresses, Lady Castlemaine, who demolished it. By the time he started to build Nonesuch, however, Henry VIII already owned the largest house in England, having added a third courtyard to Hampton Court, which he had persuaded Cardinal Wolsey to give him in 1525. It was typical of Wolsey's pretentious arrogance to build himself a palace that rivalled Richmond, but the English people were not as impressed as he may have hoped. Public opinion was summed up in a silly piece of doggerel by the satirical poet John Skelton, who had once been tutor to the king:

> *Why come you not to court?*
> *To which court,*
> *The King's court or Hampton Court?*

Henry VIII was succeeded by his three surviving children.

25. Longleat House, Wiltshire, 1572–80. The final version of Sir John Thynne's own house is the first complete great house to demonstrate the transformation of Italian and, to a lesser extent, French Renaissance architecture into a uniquely English style. The whole house looks outwards over its park, and each façade, which is symmetrical in itself, mirrors its opposite, so that the north and south sides are the same and the east façade is repeated on the west. The four bays that project forward are simplified versions of the end bays at Somerset House, their paired windows framed by flat Classical columns or pilasters. Only the elaborate cresting above the balustrade on these projections, the chimney stacks and the domed rooms on the flat lead roof break above the line of the continuous parapet.

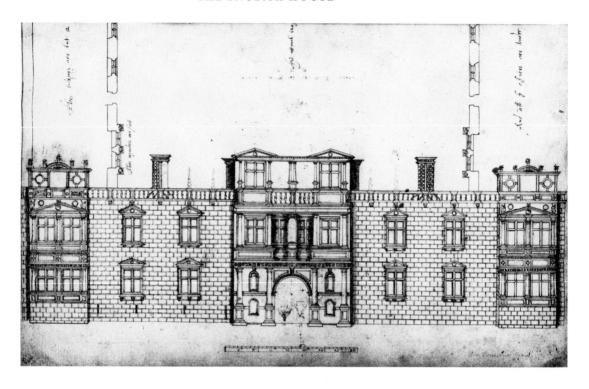

The first two hardly had a chance to do any building: Edward VI died while still a child and Mary only ruled for five years. It was during their reigns, however, that men began to build the first great houses in which the Renaissance influence was immediately apparent. In 1547, on Edward's accession, Edward Seymour, Earl of Hertford, persuaded the Privy Council to make him Lord Protector, granted himself the dukedom of Somerset and knocked down several churches in order to build a London residence on the Strand, Somerset House. In the last years of the previous reign he had fought in France with the old-fashioned English army, and he attempted to model the decoration of his house on the Classical style that he had seen there. It was replaced by the present building during the eighteenth century, but at the time it was an inevitable influence on the houses of those who served under him at court, and their houses in turn were to influence others.

In 1556, during the reign of Mary, Somerset's secretary, William Cecil, began to build Burghley House in Northamptonshire. And by then his former steward, Sir John Thynne, had started work on the first version of what was eventually to be one of the most famous 'prodigy houses', Longleat House in Wiltshire. When Somerset became Protector, Thynne had been knighted and appointed Comptroller of

26. Old Somerset House, London, 1547–52. Three of the most influential buildings in English architecture have been built on this site in the middle of London, which stretches from the banks of the Thames to the Strand. This, the first, was built for the Lord Protector, the Duke of Somerset. His steward of the household, Sir John Thynne, was at least partially responsible for the house. It was, like so many large houses of the period, built round a courtyard, but the side of the house that fronts onto the Strand shows it to be the first house in England to adapt the Classical ideas of the Renaissance to the whole façade of a house. Symmetry had already made its appearance along with odd Classical detail in the houses built during Henry VIII's reign, but here was something entirely new. Classical details like columns abound: the lower part of the central section is in the form of a triumphal arch and the four mullion and transom windows with Classical proportions and pediments on either side of the central gateway are the first of their kind in England. These windows are set in walls of dressed stone, and the positioning of the joints has been carefully worked out. The balustraded parapet conceals the roof, and only in the centre section and the two end projections does the design become over-complicated.

27. The courtyard at Burghley House, Northamptonshire, 1552–64 and 1573–87. One of the last sections of the house to be finished was the great tower surmounted by an obelisk, in the base of which there is a huge clock. The design of the tower itself is a development of the centrepiece of Somerset House, the ground and first floors both being based on the theme of a triumphal arch.

the Royal Household. He was an astute business man and so rich that when the almost completed Longleat burned down in 1567 he started again with a new plan. The final version, finished in 1580, is a perfect example of the unique English fusion of Gothic and Renaissance. The plan of the stone building is similar to a late-medieval 'castle', and on the roof there are extravagant chimneys and irregular turrets, some of which were used as 'banqueting rooms' for intimate parties after dinner. But the façades are symmetrical, the pillasters between the windows are Classical, and there are Classical statues along the Classical balustraded parapet.

Henry VIII's third surviving child, Elizabeth I, ruled from 1558 to 1603. Unlike her father, she was no builder: but she

28. Unlike Longleat, Burghley represents a struggle to achieve symmetry over a long period. On one side of the courtyard, the medieval hall and kitchen still remain, but the other three sides present different but symmetrical fronts to both courtyard and park. Longleat and Burghley are the first of the brilliantly named 'prodigy houses', being magnificent examples of prodigious size and extravagance. They are also monuments to the incredible inventiveness of their owners and their master-builders, for they have no parallel in any other country.

was a great inspirer of building in others. In the hope that she would honour them with a visit, her richest courtiers spent everything they had on houses that were splendid enough to be worthy of her, and large enough to accommodate the 150 officials and attendants who regularly travelled with her. Cecil, who became Lord Burghley and Elizabeth's Chief Secretary of State, extended Burghley House and entertained her there often – at a cost of up to £3,000 a time. After one of her early visits to Theobalds, his house in Hertfordshire, had left his own household with nowhere to sleep, he built on so much that it became the largest house in England, with five courtyards stretching over a quarter of a mile. In 1579 he wrote to another Privy Councillor, Sir Christopher Hatton, who had just built the enormous Holdenby Hall in Northamptonshire, 'God send us both long to enjoy her for whom we both mean to exceed our purses in these.'

Sir Christopher had first impressed the queen with his dancing. He was so eager to entertain her that while Holdenby was being built he bought a new house almost as big nearby, Kirby Hall, and swore that he would not even look at it until 'that holy saint might sit in it'. The building of Holdenby and the buying of Kirby ruined him financially. The queen appointed him Lord Chancellor in 1587, but the income of his high office was not enough to make him solvent. When he died in 1591 he still owed over £56,000, most of it to the 'holy saint' herself, and she had never come to stay in either of his houses. He loved her so much, however, that it may have been some consolation to him when she came to visit him on his death-bed and spent the night at the house in London which he rented.

29. Wollaton Hall, Nottinghamshire, 1580. Despite the unusual plan of Wollaton, Joseph Nash's nineteenth-century view shows it as a medieval type of hall with a screen, the details of which, however, are Classical.

Holdenby and Theobalds did not survive Oliver Cromwell. But Burghley and Kirby are still standing, and so are several other 'prodigy houses'. The most ostentatious, Wollaton Hall in Nottinghamshire, was built by Sir Francis Willoughby, a gentleman of modest pedigree who made an immense fortune in iron and coal and changed his name to Willoughby from Bugge. The ingenious design of the house was actually based on an Italian villa, but it is utterly overwhelmed by a discordant variety of pretentious decorations and devices. On the other hand, the finest 'prodigy house', Hardwick Hall in Derbyshire, was built by a woman, Bess of Hardwick.

Bess was the daughter of the squire of Hardwick. She was not born rich and she was never beautiful. But by the time she was sixty years old she had been successively widowed by Robert Barlow, a fourteen-year-old whom she married when she was thirteen and who died a few months later; Sir William Cavendish, Treasurer of the Chamber to Henry VIII, whom she persuaded to sell his land in Suffolk and buy the Chatsworth estates instead; Sir William St Loe, Grand Butler of England and Captain of the Queen's Guard; and finally, the

30. Wollaton Hall. The queen's master mason, Robert Smythson, worked on the final version of Longleat, and his epitaph in Wollaton church credits him as 'Architecter and Survayor unto the most worthy house of Wollaton with divers others of great account'. It is certainly a 'worthy' house; it is also the most eccentric and ostentatious of all the Elizabethan 'prodigy houses'. The stonework of the immensely ornate architectural details is brilliantly carved. Smythson has placed his great hall in the centre, where other Elizabethan builders would have had a courtyard, and lit it with windows in the central tower, which is further raised to accommodate a great chamber above the hall.

best catch of all, George Talbot, Earl of Shrewsbury. The last three had left her a fortune. There was only one woman in England who was richer, and that was another Bess, the queen.

Her last marriage had been bitterly acrimonious. When the earl died, she was living where she had been born, in the Old Hall at Hardwick. At once she began to build a new one. In 1597, when she was seventy-seven years old, she moved into her magnificent mansion.

Hardwick is much more compact than the other 'prodigy houses'. Apart from a few eccentricities, such as Longford Castle, which was triangular, the others were all evolutions of the late-fifteenth-century plans, extended Hs, courtyards and open-ended courtyards in the shape of a U, which with the addition of a central porch was turned into a loyal E. On the whole they were only one room thick, with rooms opening into each other in rows, and their halls ran across the houses between two wings, parallel to the front and at right-angles to the entrance. At Hardwick, however, the basic plan was a rectangle with six towers, two on each side and one at each end, and the compactness and a greater symmetry were achieved by one simple innovation: the hall was turned through ninety degrees so that it cut across the centre of the rectangle with the entrance at one end of it.

31. Hardwick Hall, Derbyshire, 1590. The most perfect and best preserved of all the great Elizabethan houses is almost certainly the work of Robert Smythson. This great house impresses solely by the deceptively simple massing of the towers as they project and recede from the lower main body of the house. The beautiful cresting on the towers, which incorporates Elizabeth Countess of Shrewsbury's initials and coronet, is the only elaborate detail.

32. The largest room on the
second floor at Hardwick is the
long gallery – one of the most
beautiful rooms in the world, if
only because of the quality of
the light. It is by no means the
longest gallery in England, but
its scale makes it much the
most impressive. A three-
storeyed terrace house would
fit comfortably into one of the
great bay windows.

From the ground upwards, the windows grow progressively larger with each floor, reflecting the importance of the
rooms beyond them. At Hardwick, the high great chamber
and other principal rooms are on the second floor. The first
floor, which also has a great chamber, was used as private
lodgings for Bess and her family, and the kitchens, nurseries
and servants' quarters are on the ground floor on either side of
the hall.

From the edge of the hall a broad stone staircase stretches off
through the house in a gentle slope and snakes upwards to the
high great chamber. This was one of the two most important
new features of the sixteenth-century house. The owners laid
great stress on the magnificence of the ceremonial route by
which guests were led from the hall to the principal room. At
Burghley, the staircase was stone-vaulted and decorated in the
French style after the manner of Imperial Rome. After its
owner first saw Holdenby, he wrote to Sir Christopher
Hatton, saying: 'I found no one thing of greater grace than
your stately ascent from your hall to your great chamber.'

Beside the high great chamber at Hardwick there is a long gallery that runs the full length of the house. This was the other important new feature. By the end of the sixteenth century, all houses of any consequence had a long gallery. The idea originated as a covered walk on the ground floor, exposed on one side like cloisters. At the beginning of the century, a second and enclosed gallery was built above it. The earliest surviving example of this was added at The Vyne in Hampshire in 1520, although the lower gallery is now enclosed. As the century progressed, however, lower galleries were gradually done away with and the galleries on the first or second floors became integral parts of the houses.

33. Grandness and simplicity characterise the main staircase at Hardwick as it rises to the state apartments on the second floor.

Although the gallery began as a place for taking exercise on a rainy day, it soon acquired other uses. It became a 'repositorie for workes of rarity in picture and other arts'. The walls were hung with portraits, not only of members of the family but also of famous men and women whose images were intended to inspire the household. In most houses the gallery was almost as richly decorated as the great chamber, and was often used instead of it for masques and plays. And when the queen came to stay, it sometimes became a dormitory for the lesser members of her retinue.

Life in the great houses changed little during the sixteenth century. Households were still large and hierarchical. Noble boys still served in them as pages – Bess employed one of her nephews at Hardwick. The great chamber was still the ceremonial focus, and the feasts that were given there were still huge. In those days the English had a reputation for the fine quality of their food, although it was often cooked by men whom the Reverend William Harrison described as 'musical-headed Frenchmen and strangers'.

There were now, however, many more rooms to be used, and in the smaller rooms there was a little less formality. Where once there had only been one parlour, there were usually two, a summer and a winter parlour. When the master of the house and his family dined alone, they often sat in one of these. There were also rooms between the great chamber and the bedchambers, known as withdrawing, or drawing, chambers, into which the occupants of the bedchambers could retire with a few chosen guests after dinner. These, too, were sometimes used for eating, and at night the personal attendants slept in them.

There was a great deal more furniture now, although it was still comparatively limited by the standards of a modern house. Chairs, chests, tables, cupboards, beds and day-beds were heavily and often quite crudely carved in Gothic or Renaissance patterns. The chairs were upholstered and covered in embroidery. There were as many pictures as tapestries on the walls, and the principal rooms of the great houses were even more elaborately decorated than their exteriors. The marble chimneypieces, the panelling, which could rise the full height of the room, the plaster friezes and the new plaster ceilings were carved, inlaid, moulded, and sometimes painted, in an astonishing variety of patterns and scenes.

The most opulent room to have survived intact is the great chamber at Gilling Castle in Yorkshire. One of the most enchanting is the hall at Montacute House in Somerset, where a plaster panel, as Classical in concept as any in the eighteenth

century, contains comical, animated, Tudor figures depicting the story of a hen-pecked husband. But the finest of them all, with its magnificent inlaid panelling and its twelve-foot painted plaster frieze of Diana the huntress and her court, is the high great chamber at Hardwick Hall.

The sixteenth-century enthusiasm for building was not limited to the rich and powerful few who could afford to build 'prodigy houses'. The lesser nobility and the now rapidly expanding middle class were also building with equal enthusiasm. Hundreds of new manor houses were built, so many that there are still several in almost every county.

The dissolution of the monasteries created a large number of beautiful but empty buildings which provided such an abundance of stone that it was used locally on cottages as well as houses. But a much more important consequence had been the disposition of their estates. Eager to join the ranks of the gentry, men who made their money in the law, commerce or government service were buying church land and building houses on it. One such was Sir William Petre, the son of a Cornish yeoman, who was appointed Secretary of State to Henry VIII and became a Privy Councillor under Elizabeth I. Ingatestone Hall, the house which he built in Essex in 1543, on land that had once belonged to a convent, was one of the first houses to have a long gallery as an integral part of its original plan.

34. Hatfield House, Hertfordshire, 1607. The embryonic H-plan of Wimbledon (see plate 36) was adopted in the house built for James I's chief minister, William Cecil's son Robert, whose brother had built Wimbledon House. Hatfield, however, departs from earlier practice in one important respect. Most houses, with the exception of those associated with Robert Smythson, had been designed to be only one room wide. Whether they were built around courtyards or in the shape of a U, an E or an H, houses from medieval times had suffered, for no very good reason, from both inconvenience and cold as a result of all the rooms being strung out one after another in endless succession. At Hatfield, the projections at either side widen to take three rooms and even in the central section the medieval arrangement of the hall was backed by an open corridor on the ground floor but a closed long gallery above.

35. Barrington Court, Somerset, 1514. Built in the reign of Henry VII, this house must have been one of the first houses built in the shape of an E, with corner turrets in the angles. It must also rate as perhaps the earliest example of a symmetrically arranged façade. It was, however, in Elizabeth's reign that the E-plan was adopted in both large and even quite modest manor houses, the central stroke of the E being no more than an entrance porch. It was a plan capable of variations while still conforming to the ideal of symmetry.

The smaller country houses were still much larger than the average manor house at the end of the previous century. In general they followed the same plans as the 'prodigy houses', but there were a few which actually preceded them: one almost symmetrical E-plan house, Barrington Court in Somerset, was built as early as 1514 by Henry VII's chamberlain, Lord Daubeney. The hall was still the central feature of the house, and the great chamber, withdrawing chambers, bedchambers, and sometimes a long gallery, were on the first floor, with the servants' quarters and storerooms above. Like the 'prodigy houses', they had grand staircases, their principal rooms had panelling and plaster ceilings, and their windows were large.

By the end of the century there were fifteen glass factories in England. Glass was being used in the little windows of

36. Wimbledon House, Surrey, 1588. Here very small projections at the back of the house gave it the shape of an embryonic H, but the pronounced projections on the entrance side with the staircase turrets in the angles look back to Barrington Court. Wimbledon was to become a model for many houses built during Elizabeth's reign and the reign of James I.

yeomen's houses. But it was still expensive, even for the rich. When the Earl of Northumberland was not in residence at Alnwick Castle, he used to have the window glass taken out to spare it the danger of being blown in by the wind.

The exteriors of the smaller country houses were always much more obviously Gothic. A few, such as Brereton Hall in Cheshire or Barlborough Hall in Derbyshire, looked like miniature 'prodigy houses'. But most of the builders were content with symmetry, pillastered porches and one or two simple Renaissance decorations. Their houses were more restrained, more dignified, more English.

Some new houses were the result of conversions. Castles, even real ones, were converted, their defensive walls pierced with windows. But perhaps the most successful conversion was carried out by Sir William Sharington, Vice Treasurer of the Bristol Mint, who embezzled the funds to finance the purchase and conversion of Lacock Abbey in Wiltshire. Sir William built a long gallery over the medieval cloisters and a second courtyard beyond the gatehouse; and on the south front he concealed the irregular roofline with a balustraded parapet and added an octagonal tower at one end. The work began in 1540 and came to an abrupt halt in 1549, when Sir William was arrested and the property confiscated. Fortunately, however, in the following year, Lady Sharington was able to secure his release and raise enough money to buy back the abbey and complete the conversion.

Many older houses were extended. Long galleries and other rooms were added at Knole and Haddon. And it was an extension amounting to a metamorphosis that produced the most famous half-timbered house in England, Little Moreton Hall in Cheshire. This was a simple medieval manor house in 1559 when William Moreton added another wing, hexagonal bays and a gatehouse. And then, in 1580, his son made it magically top-heavy by building on a second storey with an extraordinary long gallery. The plaster panels between the structural timbers contain other, decorative timbers, covering the façades of the house in a mass of black and white patterns.

38. The Great Staircase at Knole, Kent, 1605. The open well type of staircase was developed in the first years of the seventeenth century. The one at Knole is the most beautiful because it is comparatively restrained. In some other houses the complexity of the carving borders on an ostentatious display of craftsmanship. Here the shape of the turned balusters is repeated in paint on the walls.

37. Detail from the Somerset House conference, 1604. The number and huge size of the windows in the great 'prodigy houses' resulted in the establishment of glassworks in England: by 1589 there were fifteen factories. Glass was still extremely expensive but not the rare commodity it had been when people bequeathed their windows in their wills. Small panes only were used and held in place by lead within a wrought-iron frame. Only a small section of the frame was made to open.

39. Little Moreton Hall, Cheshire, 1559 and 1580. The first large extension to the original medieval manor was made in 1559, but much decorative detail must have been incorporated at the time the top-floor gallery was added in 1580. This structurally unnecessary and slightly absurd amount of timber decoration was characteristic of a number of houses built in the west of England during the latter part of Elizabeth's reign and during the reign of James I. The main structural divisions are typical of timber-framed houses in the west of England.

It is an exuberant Elizabethan fantasy. And yet, even here, there is a hint of a Renaissance influence. On the internal walls at either end of the long gallery there are painted plaster figures that might have come from an Italian picture.

Half-timbering was still the most common form of construction in the centre of the towns. In the west of England the wattle and daub panels were still whitewashed and the timbers were still coated in tar, but in the south-east, where it became common to fill panels with brick, the timbers were left untreated to blend with it. In the first half of the century, the town houses changed little, although they extended further to the rear. But during the reign of Queen Elizabeth I, some rich merchants expanded their houses by buying a neighbour's and knocking the two together, and some built new houses which took up as much street frontage as three or four old ones. One of the largest to have survived is a four-bayed, symmetrical mansion in Shrewsbury which was built at the end of the century by a wool merchant called Robert Ireland, and which was known in the following century as Ireland's Folly. There are several other houses of this period in Shrewsbury, and there are several in Chester, Exeter and Newark, but in most towns those that were not replaced or burned, or destroyed by bombs in the Second World War, have since been demolished to make way for wider roads.

The half-timbered house is usually regarded as typical of the Tudor period, but in the countryside it was actually much rarer than it had been in the previous centuries. There had been no replanting during the Middle Ages. Timber was becoming scarce. Where there were still trees tall enough to provide big beams, the shipbuilders had first call on them. The price rose dramatically. Cottages and yeomen's houses used as few timbers as possible, and in some areas it was cheaper to build in brick or even stone. The decorative woodwork at Little Moreton Hall is almost as much a symbol of wealth as its windows.

The cottages, farmhouses and yeomen's houses varied considerably in size and materials from region to region, and it

40. Farmhouse near Stoke Poges, Buckinghamshire. The house shown in this drawing of 1798 by Hendrik de Cort shows brick chimney stacks, brick gable-end walls and brick infilling to the timber framing of the front wall. During the seventeenth century and later, brick was often used to replace the old wattle and daub infilling when it rotted away. The casement windows are glazed, but this drawing was made one year after a traveller around England had noted: 'Glass is at length introduced into windows of most cottages.'

was during the sixteenth century that regional styles began to emerge. In the south-east, the yeomen's houses and farm-houses were like little medieval manor houses, with a hall running between two wings. Elsewhere they were usually rectangular. By now most of the cottages in the south-east had fireplaces and chimneys. Some were two-storeyed and built in rows. In Kent some of these had tile cladding on the outside of their upper storeys. In East Anglia many of the timber frames were completely covered over with plaster which was decorated with mouldings known as pargeting. In the sheep-farming areas of the north-west, the little stone houses had wooden 'spinning galleries' on the first floor. But there were still plenty of cruck cottages and houses with no more than a bower for the family, and in some areas, such as Cornwall, most of the labourers were still living in cob huts without a window or a chimney.

Many of the poorest inhabitants of the country migrated to the towns in search of work, creating overcrowding and adding to the squalor. Little had changed. The Dutch human-

41. Detail from The Wedding Feast in Bermondsey by J. Hoefnagel, c. 1570. The in this scene show the use of brick walls for simple houses, although timber framing has been used in the gable-end walls for the upper storey. Both thatch and clay tiles are depicted as roofing material. Many of the windows are not glazed and at this period such houses would only have had shutters on the inside.

ist, Erasmus, who lived in England for a while, was disgusted by the smaller town houses: 'The floors are made of clay and are covered with layers of rushes, constantly replenished, so that the bottom layer remains for twenty years harbouring spittle, vomit, the urine of dogs and men, the dregs of beer, the remnants of fish and other nameless filth.' Efforts to clean up the streets were usually as futile as ever. Plagues were still frequent and there were a few new diseases as well: 'sweating sickness', smallpox and syphilis. Washing went out of fashion. Henry VIII closed all the 'stews', or public bath houses, in London on the grounds that they were brothels, which they were. In private houses the cost of wood made hot baths an expensive luxury, and cold baths were considered to be dangerous for the health.

There was, however, one advance in sanitary engineering. In 1596 Queen Elizabeth's witty godson, Sir John Harrington, invented the water-closet. Few people adopted the idea, but that was probably just as well. Sir John had omitted two important elements. The drain pipe was not ventilated and it had no U-bend, or trap, with the result that the sewer gas drifted back into the house. The pipes were still unventilated when water-closets became common, which is why the nineteenth-century English were always complaining about the stink of drains.

42. This fifteenth-century house at Clare, Suffolk, was pargeted at the end of the seventeenth century. In medieval times pargeting was another word for plastering; it was only later that it was used to describe decorative plasterwork. Here the earlier timber-framed house has been plastered over with the decoration applied on top. This form of decoration, most commonly found in East Anglia, derived from skills that the plasterer had used on the ceilings inside the larger houses.

The only general progress in the design of privies was towards greater comfort. The cold stone garderobes were replaced by stool-houses, each of which contained a wooden close-stool, which was like a large commode. Sir William Petre installed five of these at Ingatestone. And he also built an elaborate system of drains, but this was by no means usual. The builders of large houses in both town and country were much more interested in display than practicalities.

The 'builders', even of the largest houses, were the men and women who paid for them and lived in them. There were as yet no real architects. Decorations were copied from Flemish pattern books. Masons turned to their employers for detailed instructions. A letter has survived which the master mason at Burghley wrote to Cecil about the windows, asking him to 'draw your meaning how and after what fashion you would have them to be made in all points'.

There were, however, surveyors who took charge of the building, and some of these men described themselves as architects. One of them, John Shute, was sent to Italy in 1550 by the Duke of Northumberland, and on his return he published *First and Chief Groundes of Architecture*, the earliest book on the subject to be printed in English. But he was a theorist, a critic and a bit of a philosopher, not a real practising architect. Another, John Thorpe, left a large collection of drawings and plans, but most of these were designs of existing houses. The nearest to a real architect was Robert Smythson. Smythson had helped with the design when he was working at Longleat as master mason, and he went on to design the plans of Wollaton and Hardwick. But even he did not have the responsibilities of an architect. He still took detailed instructions. The blame for Wollaton and the praise for Hardwick should rest as much with his patrons as with Smythson.

Nevertheless, by the end of the century, the educated patrons were aware that talented surveyors and pattern books were not enough. England was ready for the first real architect of her own. And it so happened that while Smythson was working at Wollaton and Hardwick, a clothworker's son was growing up in London who was to fill that role with genius.

CHAPTER 4

The First Architect

43. Portrait of Inigo Jones by R. Van Voerst after Van Dyck.

THE clothmaker's son, Inigo Jones, was born on 15 July 1573. Very little is known about his early life. It is said that as a boy he was apprenticed to a joiner in St Paul's churchyard; and at some time before the turn of the century, a rich patron, who may have been the Earl of Pembroke, was persuaded by the quality of his sketches to send him to Italy to study painting. From Italy he went on to Denmark, apparently at the invitation of King Christian IV, whose sister Anne was married to James I of England, and it has since been suggested that while he was there he designed the palaces of Rosenborg and Frederiksborg, but King Christian was himself a designer and it seems more likely that at this stage of his career Jones was simply working for the king as a draughtsman.

The story becomes clearer, however, after his return to England in 1605. Under Queen Anne's patronage he became the leading theatrical designer of his day. He created extravagant sets and costumes for the masques of Ben Jonson, he introduced movable scenery, and he has been credited with the invention of the proscenium arch as well. At the same time he designed his first known building, the New Exchange in the Strand, which was completed in 1608 and demolished during the eighteenth century. And in 1610 the queen secured him the appointment of Surveyor of Works to her elder son, Henry, Prince of Wales.

It should have been a great opportunity. The 16-year-old Henry was already recognised as a burgeoning 'Renaissance Prince'. Dignified, discerning, intelligent, athletic and extremely popular, he was far more able than his younger brother Charles – and he was much too politically astute to alienate a parliament with haughty intransigence. But Jones was never to receive a commission from him, for two years later, after a hard game of tennis, Prince Henry tore off his shirt, dived into the Thames, caught typhoid fever and died of it. For Inigo Jones it was only a setback: for the English it was even more of a tragedy than they realised.

In the following year, 1613, on the death of the king's Surveyor of Works, Inigo Jones was appointed to succeed him. Before he took up the office, however, he obtained permission to return to Italy with Thomas Howard, second Earl of Arundel, the first Englishman to build a great collection of works of art. For the next nineteen months Jones travelled round the Italian cities with the earl and countess, on one of the first of those grand tours which were soon to be essential to the education of an English gentleman, and he took with him a book which he had brought back from his earlier visit, *Quattro Libri dell' Architettura* by Andrea Palladio.

Of all the great Italian Renaissance architects, Palladio had been the one who adhered most faithfully to the precepts of Classical Roman architecture. In the opening sentence of his book he wrote, 'My natural inclination leading me from my very infancy to the study of architecture, I resolved to apply myself to it, and because I was of the opinion that the ancient Romans far excelled all who have come after them, as in many other things so particularly in building, I proposed to myself Vitruvius as my master and guide, he being the only ancient author that remains extant on this subject.'

Palladio's four volumes were a theoretical treatise on proportion in architecture based on the principles laid down by Vitruvius, who had written ten volumes in the middle of the first century B.C. The Romans had derived their designs from Greek architecture. They had evolved their own versions of the Greek columns, often using more than one type on one building, and they had developed their own more elaborate decorations, but they had regarded the Greek rules of proportion and symmetry as sacred. Vitruvius had emphasised these rules, detailing the precise measurements and methods by which the proportions could be calculated, and Palladio had repeated them with equal emphasis. In his own work he had always obeyed them, although, like the Romans, he had developed his own decorative style.

Towards the end of his life, Palladio's decorations had begun to show symptoms of the more fluid Baroque style, and in the thirty-three years since his death in 1580, Baroque had become the dominant fashion in Italy. But Inigo Jones was more interested in ancient Roman buildings than he was in contemporary Italian architecture. He met Palladio's pupil Scamozzi, he visited the Roman sites, measuring the ruins and comparing them with Palladio's sketches, and his copy of Palladio's book, which is now in Worcester College, Oxford, is filled with the notes that he made at the time. Many years later he wrote in the same vein as Palladio:

Being naturally inclined in my younger days to study the arts of design, I passed into foreign parts to converse with the great masters thereof in Italy; where I applied myself to search out the ruins of those ancient buildings, which, in

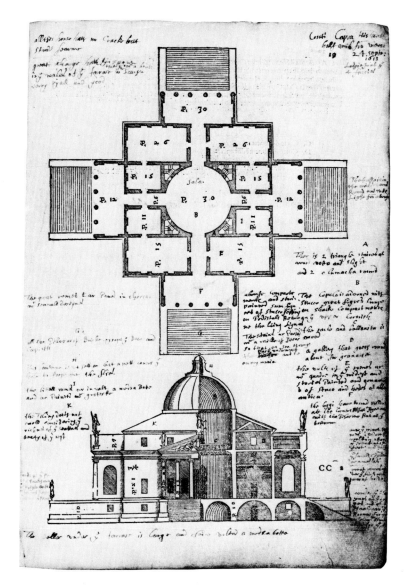

44. A page from Inigo Jones's copy of Palladio's *Four Books of Architecture,* first published in Venice in 1570. Jones annotated his copy during his last visit to Italy in 1613–14.

despite of time itself and violence of barbarians, are yet remaining. Having satisfied myself in these, and returning to my native country, I applied my mind more particularly to the study of architecture.

In 1616, after his return to England, Inigo Jones designed a new house at Greenwich for the queen. The work was abandoned on her death in 1619, but in the same year he designed a new Banqueting House for the Palace of Whitehall in London. Completed entirely under his supervision in 1622, at a cost of £15,000, it was the first Classical building in England. The roof is hidden behind a balustrade, the façades,

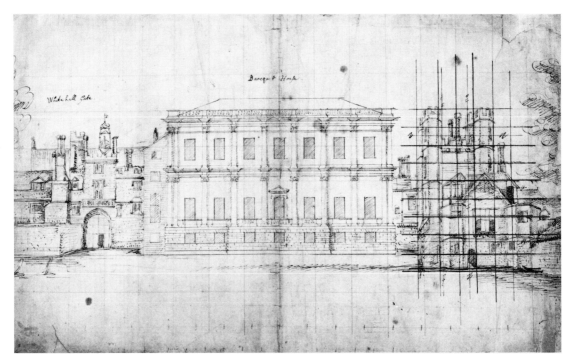

45. The Banqueting House, Whitehall, 1619–22. This was almost certainly the first Classical building to stand finished in England and in a very prominent position in the capital. Together with the Lodgings built for Prince Charles, the future Charles I, at Newmarket, it represents the first fruits of Jones's study of Italian buildings, in particular those of Andrea Palladio. It was refaced in 1772, when the stone was found to be weathering badly, and the mullion and transom windows were replaced by Georgian sash windows. Although it is not a house, and was designed for banquets and the masques for which Jones had designed sets and costumes before he turned to architecture, its influence on the design of houses was considerable. Its full impact was delayed by the Civil War and only reached its peak a hundred years later.

like the plan itself, are rectangular, and the two rows of rectangular windows, which have since been replaced by sash windows, were originally wooden-framed casements with large, leaded panes, divided by vertical mullions and horizontal transoms into squares at the top and rectangles below. All the proportions are precisely as Palladio dictated. But Inigo Jones did not imitate Palladio, any more than Palladio imitated Vitruvius or Vitruvius the Greeks. He adapted the Classical idiom to the English environment, and the style and the restrained Classical decoration are entirely his own. The windows are larger than in Italian buildings to allow for the English lack of light. The rows of pilasters and engaged columns between them are not exact reproductions of Greek or Roman versions: on the upper level they are his own composite, and below they are his own version of the Ionic style.

Despite its two rows of windows, the interior above the basement is one huge double-cubed hall, and as in all Jones's buildings it is much more elaborately decorated than the exterior.

> In all designing of ornaments [he wrote] one must first design the ground plan as it is for use. . . . For as outwardly every wise man carries himself gravely in public places, yet inwardly has imagination and fire which sometimes flies out unrestrained, just as nature sometimes flies out to delight or

amuse us, to move us to laughter, contemplation or even horror; so in architecture the outward ornament is to be solid, proportionable according to rule, masculine and unaffected.

His first ten years as surveyor of the king's works were the busiest of Inigo Jones's career, but, sadly, very little that he designed has survived. Out of his several additions to royal palaces, the only one still standing is the Queen's Chapel at St James's Palace, now the chapel of Marlborough House. Over its altar he built the first Venetian window in England, a three-piece window with an arch over the centre and rectangles on either side. The lodge that he built for Prince Charles at Newmarket was destroyed during the following century. He rebuilt St Paul's Cathedral, but it was damaged beyond repair in the Great Fire of London. He remodelled the north side of the courtyard at Kirby and built his only new country house, Stoke Park in Northamptonshire, the first in England to be flanked by Palladian pavilions, but the central block was probably finished by another architect and all that remains of it today are the pavilions. He also took part in several town-planning schemes. He designed the first square in London on the Duke of Bedford's land in Covent Garden, with the duke's

46. The Prince's Lodgings, Newmarket, Suffolk, 1619–22. This design for a hunting lodge was of more immediate importance as an influence on houses. With the exception of the arrangement of the windows, where the first-floor window heights dominate those above and below, this house can stand as the model for countless later seventeenth- and early eighteenth-century houses. It was certainly seen by one Dutch architect and could well have influenced Dutch Palladian buildings like the Mauritzhuis at The Hague. The central feature, with its pediment set low against the steeply pitched roof, the dormer windows with their differing pediments and the quoins at each break in the façade all reappear again in both great houses and small manor houses all over England.

garden on one side, arcaded houses opposite and at one end, and the church of St Paul at the other end, fronted by England's first Tuscan portico. The church is still there, but even that was restored after a fire in 1795.

In 1635, however, Jones completed the Queen's House at Greenwich for Charles I's queen, Henrietta Maria. The house was built on a site by the river, but the Dover road ran across the site and the bulk of the park was on the other side of it. If the house had been built on the park side, the queen would have had to cross the road to reach it when she arrived on the river in her barge; if it had been built on the river side, she would have had to cross the road to reach her park. To overcome this, Inigo Jones built the house in two rectangular blocks with the road between them and joined them in the centre in the shape of an H with a block that ran across the road on the first floor like a bridge.

The exterior of the house is utterly simple, relying entirely on its proportions for its beauty. The only break in the façades is the loggia on the park side, derived from Palladio's at the Villa Pisani near Vicenza. Inside the front door the elegant Italianate hall is a forty-foot cube rising the full height of the house with a gallery running round it on the first floor. The circular 'Tulip Staircase', named after its graceful wrought-iron decorations, which stands beyond a door on the left, was the first in England to be built without a newel, or supporting column. It has, as Jones put it, 'a vacuum in the middle': the ends of the steps are embedded in the wall and the whole staircase spirals upwards, delicately and spectacularly, without any visible means of support.

The only known house which was similar to Jones's was the Italianate Newington House in Oxfordshire, which was built by the high sheriff, Walter Dunch, soon after 1630. Elsewhere patrons and their surveyors were still building in a mixture of Classical and Gothic styles. But they had lost the confident exuberance which had fused the two styles successfully. In 1607 Lord Burghley's second son, Robert Cecil, later Earl of Salisbury, built the huge, self-conscious Hatfield House in Hertfordshire. In 1616, when Inigo Jones was starting work on the Queen's House, the surveyor at Hatfield, Robert Lyminge, began to build Blickling Hall in Norfolk, a brick house with so little Classical decoration that it was almost an evolution of early Tudor houses like Layer Marney. At Bolsover Castle in Derbyshire, Robert Smythson's son John returned to the old-style castle plan in the house that he built for Sir Charles Cavendish, the third son of Bess of Hardwick. The symmetry was destroyed by a striking keep at one end,

47. The Queen's House, Greenwich, 1616–35, was built as two houses on either side of a main road and bridged at first-floor level. Two further bridges were added by Jones's pupil and nephew by marriage, John Webb, giving the house its present-day appearance of a single building.

49. (*Right*) Raynham Hall, Norfolk, 1622–39. The great chamber lies behind the columned, temple-like centrepiece (see plate 50). The plasterwork of the ceiling was built up on a timber core and dates from about 1660. The painting within the compartments is by William Kent.

48. The Tulip Staircase at the Queen's House. Jones's most remarkable achievement inside the house was the cantilevered staircase with its carved stone treads and beautiful wrought-iron balustrade. At the point where the stairs reach the ground floor from the basement, the wrought-iron work becomes more elaborate and the tulips which give the staircase its name are brought into the design.

and in the building which he added for Sir Charles's son William, his combination of Gothic and Classical features ended in a clash rather than a fusion. Most patrons were still so indifferent to Classicism that after Bolsover was completed, in 1633, Charles I was invited to a masque in its garden by Ben Jonson, *Love's Welcome at Bolsover*, in which Classical architecture was ridiculed and the architect of the Queen's House was caricatured as a surveyor called Iniquius Vitruvium.

By then, however, many of the London merchants were turning to a purer version of the Dutch Renaissance style, which had been introduced by a new wave of Protestant Flemish refugees who had fled from further Catholic persecution. One of the earliest examples of this style had been a comparatively large house, Raynham Hall in Norfolk, which was designed by its owner, Sir Roger Townshend, in 1622, but the medium-sized houses which the merchants built in the south-east were more restrained and were similar to the Dutch House at Kew in Surrey, now known as Kew Palace, which

50. (*Left*) One of the more eccentric houses of Charles I's reign, Raynham Hall was the combined effort of Sir Roger Townshend and his master mason, whom he had taken with him to the continent. The garden front, tidied up by William Kent about a hundred years later, now presents the result Townshend and his mason may have been aiming at. The gables have a Dutch appearance, but similar gables appear on Palladio's Villa Barbaro at Maser, which also has a central pedimented feature breaking through the line of the roof.

52. (*Right*) The Dutch House at Kew, Surrey, 1631, is shown in the background of this painting by P. Mercier of Frederick, Prince of Wales, and his three sisters. At Raynham the decorative architectural details were carried out in stone. Here they are all in brick and bear witness to the skills being developed by the Flemish master bricklayers. At a time when there was virtually only one architect in England, the design of houses such as this was still being entrusted to master craftsmen, with or without the assistance of their patrons.

51. (*Left, below*) Blickling Hall, Norfolk, 1616–24. An early nineteenth-century painting showing the brick when rendered. The revolution in architecture that Inigo Jones brought about single-handedly is dramatically demonstrated by comparing Blickling with the Queen's House. Both were begun in the same year. Although work was protracted on the Queen's House, the Banqueting House in Whitehall and the Prince's Lodgings were finished two years before Blickling Hall, and Blickling's owner, the Lord Chief Justice, Sir Henry Hobart, would have seen both, as the road to his Norfolk house went through Newmarket.

was built for a Flemish merchant, Samuel Fortrey, in 1631. The Dutch House was one of the first in which Flemish craftsmen used their own bonding methods, together with a softer brick in which pilasters and columns could be carved after they had been built.

Although Charles I may have laughed at Ben Jonson's masque, he was Inigo Jones's greatest admirer and patron, having retained him in the office of Surveyor of Works. Once he had persuaded his Lord Chamberlain, Philip, fourth Earl of Pembroke, to build a new south front at Wilton House in Wiltshire, he recommended Jones as the architect. At the time, Jones was too busy with the king's work to accept the

commission, but he suggested instead that it should be given to a Huguenot called Isaac de Caus, and according to the unreliable gossip John Aubrey, de Caus did nothing without Jones's approval. 'King Charles I did love Wilton above all other places,' wrote Aubrey, 'and came thither every summer. It was he that did put Philip, Earl of Pembroke, upon making the magnificent garden and grotto, and to new build that side of the house that fronts the garden with two stately pavilions at each end, all al Italiano.'

The new building was intended to contain separate apartments for the king and queen, but in 1640 the king dismissed his Lord Chamberlain. The earl completed the building to a more modest plan, and two years later, on the outbreak of the Civil War, he joined the Parliamentarian army.

The Civil War brought a halt to Inigo Jones's career. He was a Royalist, and worse, he was a Catholic. Deprived of his

53. Wilton House, Wiltshire, 1632 and 1649. Much of Isaac de Caus's magnificent garden front, which was to be the model for at least four houses during the eighteenth century, was rebuilt by John Webb after it had been damaged by fire in 1648.

54. The whole centre of the garden front at Wilton is taken up by the double-cube room, which is 30 feet in width and height and 60 feet in length. The eighteenth-century furniture is by William Kent.

office, he took refuge at Basing House in Hampshire until it was captured by Oliver Cromwell in 1645. In the following year Parliament fined him and seized his property; but he was later pardoned by the House of Lords, and in 1649, the year in which Charles I was executed outside the Banqueting House, Jones was working at Wilton with his pupil and nephew by marriage, John Webb, rebuilding the south front which had been damaged by fire. It was then that Webb designed the towers, or 'stately pavilions', and it was then that Inigo Jones completed his last great masterpiece, Wilton's magnificent double-cube room. He died on 21 June 1652.

For the next thirty years his Classical influence spread slowly through the work of his pupil and a handful of followers, in particular Hugh May, who had served with Charles II during his exile in Europe, and Roger Pratt, a Norfolk gentleman who had spent six years travelling in France, Italy and the Netherlands during the Civil War, in order, as he said himself, 'To avoid the storm and give myself some convenient education.' Most of the houses that they built have since been demolished or replaced, but, like Inigo Jones's, they were to set the fashion for generations of houses that followed.

After the Restoration, Webb was bitterly disappointed when Charles II refused to install him as Jones's successor in the office of Surveyor of Works and appointed the unpopular Irish poet and lawyer John Denham in his place. He pleaded in vain that the king's father had commanded Inigo Jones to educate him in the study of architecture so that he might serve him in 'the said office', and he went on to point out the advantages of a qualified architect: 'Mr Denham may possibly, as most gentry in England at this day, have some knowledge of the Theory of Architecture; but nothing of the practice, so that he must of necessity have another at His Majesty's charges to do his business; whereas Mr Webb himself designs, orders and directs . . . without any other man's assistance.'

Nevertheless, Webb worked for the king at Greenwich, building the first block of the new palace which was later to become the Royal Naval Hospital, and adding the two bridges to the Queen's House which turned its upper floor into a rectangle. Elsewhere he built several houses, including Amesbury in Wiltshire, which was to become one of the models for the first villas of the following century, and it now seems likely that he was responsible for the design of Ashdown House in Berkshire, combining Jones's Classicism with the Dutch style in a vertical rectangle flanked by low pavilions. He also remodelled the garden front at The Vyne and made it

55. The double-cube room at Wilton, like the single-cube room adjoining it, was designed by Jones and Webb. It is one of the most lavishly decorated rooms in any English house. The white and gold decorations on the walls were specially designed to incorporate portraits by Van Dyck.

the first house in England to have a tall portico in the centre. During the eighteenth century, when country gentlemen believed that the Romans had used porticos as a sign of rank, they became as much a status symbol as crenellations had been in the fifteenth century.

Hugh May followed Jones closely in his interiors, although his exteriors were more Dutch in appearance. Eltham Lodge in Kent, which he completed in 1665 for Sir John Shaw, a rich vintner who had assisted the king during his exile, was based on the Mauritzhuis in The Hague. It is the only one of May's houses to have survived, but it is also the one that was to be the model for a large number of smaller country houses during the reigns of William and Mary and Queen Anne.

Roger Pratt, on the other hand, followed Jones most closely in his exteriors. His masterpiece was Clarendon House in

56. (*Left*) Ashdown House, Berkshire, *c.* 1650. The date and architect of this house are uncertain, but it has been attributed to John Webb.

57. Eltham Lodge, Kent, 1665. Hugh May's only surviving house bears a close resemblance to the Mauritzhuis in The Hague. Like other gentlemen architects who served there with the English Court in exile, May had been inspired by the Dutch Palladian style, which had first appeared during the 1630s, and which may have been derived from Inigo Jones's house at Newmarket.

London, which was completed in 1667 for the Lord Chancellor, Edward Hyde, Earl of Clarendon. It was demolished after only eighteen years, but it was widely imitated, most closely at Belton House in Lincolnshire. The diarist John Evelyn, whom Pratt had befriended in Italy, described it as 'without hyperbolies, the best contrived, the most useful, graceful and magnificent house in England'.

Pratt's most significant house, however, was his first, Coleshill House in Berkshire, which was demolished unnecess-

58. (*Above left*) Clarendon House, London, 1664–7. Roger Pratt was second only to Inigo Jones in influencing the design of subsequent generations of houses. His Clarendon House stood for only eighteen years, but in its prominent position in Piccadilly it formed a model for many others. The high-pitched roof and pedimented central feature echo Jones's lodge at Newmarket.

59. (*Left*) Belton House in Lincolnshire, built twenty years later, was probably modelled on Clarendon House.

60. (*Above*) The Vyne, Hampshire, altered 1654. The portico, the first on any house in England, was added by John Webb, whose other alterations to this early-Tudor house included a new fireplace for the earliest surviving long gallery.

61. Coleshill, Berkshire, 1650. Like all his houses, and like Newington, from which it was almost certainly derived, Pratt's first house was raised on a semi-basement and had what he called a 'double-pile' plan, in which two ranges of rooms were divided by a corridor. Pratt consulted Jones about the design, but unlike Jones, and again following the example of Newington, he gave equal emphasis to both the principal floors.

62. Newington House, near Oxford, c. 1630. A reconstruction by Michael Pickwoad of the original house before it was remodelled in the eighteenth century. Built by Walter Dunch, whose family was later related to Pratt's by marriage, Newington may have been based on a drawing of a palace in Genoa by Rubens, whose patron, Tobias Palavicini, was also related to Dunch by marriage. Pratt matriculated at nearby Oxford soon after the house was completed.

arily after a fire in 1952. Although larger, it was very similar to Newington, which Pratt would have seen while a student at Oxford. It had a minimum of external decoration, and the only vertical lines in the long rectangular façades were created by the windows, which were spaced further apart in the centre to mark the location of the principal rooms. Pratt designed the house for his cousin, Sir George Pratt, in 1650, and during the last two years of his life Inigo Jones visited the site to advise him.

Like many other gentlemen who were to return after him from more honourable exile with the heir to the throne, Pratt admired the balanced interiors of the new continental houses, and at Coleshill he adapted these plans to the changing needs of the English country gentleman. It was what he called a 'double-pile' house, divided internally, like Newington, by corridors which ran through the centre from end to end on each floor with doors opening off them into the rooms on either side, so that it was now possible to reach any main room without going through any of the others. And it was also the first house in England to have an entirely symmetrical interior. There was a servants' hall in the basement beside the kitchens, and the hall itself, which rose through two storeys, became no more than an impressive entrance hall, or vestibule, with England's first double staircase rising up either side of it to a gallery. The great chamber and parlour, which in earlier houses had stood one above the other at the side of the hall, were moved to the centre of the house beyond it as a great dining chamber and a great parlour. On either side of these there were rooms which could be used as parlours, withdrawing chambers or bedchambers, each of which had two little rooms beyond it at the edge of the house, a closet and a servant's room. Flanking the hall, on the other side of the central corridors, there were identical sets of rooms; and at the ends of the corridors, where doors opened into the servants' rooms, there were back staircases which ran down to the basement and up to the attic, allowing the servants to go about their duties unobserved.

There was a decline in the social status of servants during the seventeenth century. After the Civil War the younger sons of gentlemen went into commerce, the law or the army, rather than service in a great house. Noblemen no longer sent their sons to serve as pages in the houses of their equals, preferring instead to educate them at home or at a school. There were still a few great lords who maintained large and well-bred households, but most households were smaller, and their masters were glad to save money by raising low-born servants in the hierarchy and paying them smaller wages for the services

63. Wisbech Castle, Cambridgeshire, *c.* 1654. This contemporary painting shows the influence of Newington and Coleshill on the much less sophisticated work of provincial builders.

which had previously been performed by expensive gentlemen. Yeomen replaced gentlemen as stewards. Butlers took over the combined roles of the yeoman of the pantry and the buttery. Some of the footmen, who ran or walked beside horses or carriages, were brought into the houses to wait at the upper servants' table in the servants' hall or the steward's room, and by the end of the century they were serving under the butler in the great chamber at dinner, which was by then being eaten at three o'clock in the afternoon.

Since women earned far less than men, many more of them were now taken on to serve in the most menial capacities as chambermaids, parlourmaids and kitchenmaids. When the house was full of guests, 'chairwomen' were hired by the day to help out in the kitchens and the laundry. Housekeepers were engaged to supervise the women; and it also became the housekeeper's duty to act as a guide to any ladies and

64. Tredegar, Monmouthshire, *c.* 1665. The only large house of the period that still retains its mullion and transom windows, Tredegar gives a good impression of what the others looked like before their windows were replaced by sash windows during the eighteenth century.

gentlemen of rank who might call at the house and ask to be shown over it.

In Coleshill and the houses that were built after it, the personal attendants, who might still be the sons and daughters of yeomen, waited and slept in the servants' rooms, while the lesser servants slept in the basement and the attic and were kept out of the way as much as possible. Their masters and mistresses no longer felt inclined to live their lives surrounded by them, and they preferred to be oblivious to their disagreeable but essential duties. Houses no longer had privy shafts in their walls. The family and their guests used chamber pots and close-stools, which were kept in the servants' rooms. If there had been no back stairs and corridors, the wretched servants who had the duty of emptying them in the cesspit far from the house would have had to carry them through the other rooms and down the grand staircase first.

After the Great Fire of London in 1666, Charles II appointed Roger Pratt as one of the commissioners responsible for replanning the city and knighted him afterwards for his services. Hugh May was another, and the third, and most famous, was Christopher Wren.

Wren had just returned from Paris, where he had met the Italian Baroque architects Bernini and Guarini. Although his first building, the chapel of Pembroke College, Cambridge, had been entirely in Jones's Classical tradition, the many churches, palaces and public buildings which he was now to design became increasingly Baroque, culminating in the completion of the Royal Naval Hospital at Greenwich; and it was the style of these that was to be the greatest influence on a new generation of 'prodigy houses'. With its movement, com-

65. Tring Manor House, Hertfordshire, *c.* 1669. Tring is the earliest of the three or four houses which can be ascribed with any certainty to Sir Christopher Wren, who, like Jones before him, was far too occupied with Royal Works to take on private commissions in the country.

66. Winslow Hall, Buckinghamshire, 1699. It is possible that Wren's Winslow was the first new private house to be designed to take the recently introduced sash windows.

plexity and grandeur, its sensuous twisted columns, scrolls and broken pediments, the Baroque style was more appealing to the ostentation of those builders who employed it than Jones's calm and static Classicism. Yet Wren himself built few houses, and those that he did build were in the Dutch tradition. Although he has been credited at some time or other with the design of almost every house built during his lifetime, the only two with which he has any certain connection are Tring Manor in Hertfordshire, which has since been altered out of all recognition, and Winslow Hall in Buckinghamshire. In a career that included reorganising the office of Royal Works and working on St Paul's Cathedral, ten university buildings, seven major public buildings, five royal palaces and fifty-two city churches, he can hardly have had time for much else.

Unlike Wren, Inigo Jones was by no means prolific. His immediate followers were few, and little of his work has survived. But he was not just the first English architect or even the first great English architect: he was the most influential of them all. A visitor who had seen Georgian houses but knew nothing of architectural history might easily look at the Queen's House in Greenwich, dwarfed in the distance between the blocks of the Royal Hospital, and imagine that it had been built a hundred years after them instead of more than sixty years before.

On his second visit to Italy, Inigo Jones had ignored the fashion for Baroque, turning instead to the Roman ruins and choosing Palladio as his guide, and when he came back to England he had planted the seeds of his own Classical, Palladian architecture – total symmetry and proportion, rectangular windows, Venetian windows, villas, porticos, pediments and pavilions. Those seeds had little chance to spread during the Civil War and the Commonwealth that followed, and after that, for a while, they were overshadowed by the new enthusiasm for Baroque. But in the end they were to blossom everywhere, in villages, whole towns, great palaces and tiny cottages, and they were to spread across the world to America, Russia, India, the West Indies, the Far East and even back to their source to the Greek island of Corfu. When the brief season of Baroque was over, they were to flourish for more than a hundred years in the golden age of English architecture.

CHAPTER 5

Designed to Impress

THE decline in the social status of servants during the seventeenth century was not to be matched by any significant decline in the size of great houses or the formality of the social life within them. After the Restoration, the richest men were again building on a scale that was magnificent enough to reflect their sense of their own importance and large enough to accommodate a visit from their monarch: and since Charles II had modelled his court on the French court of Louis XIV, they laid out the rooms of their new houses in accordance with the new customs and etiquette, basing their designs on the French châteaux, in particular Vaux-le-Vicomte, which had been completed by King Louis's Finance Minister, Nicholas Fouquet, towards the end of Charles's exile.

In the early Middle Ages, French houses had been exactly the same as English houses – halls with great chambers at one end of them. But since then their evolution had been different. Where the English gentry and nobility had withdrawn from the hall to the great chamber, their French counterparts had stayed in the hall and moved out their servants and retainers instead. The French chamber had remained a bed-sitting-room and had continued to be used as such even after the addition of other rooms. In the symmetrical Italian plan at Vaux-le-Vicomte, a vestibule led to a central hall, which was known as a *grand salon*, and on either side of this there were matching sets of rooms, or *appartements*. The first rooms in each of these, which in England would have been withdrawing chambers, were simply elegantly decorated antechambers, or waiting rooms. The *chambres* beyond, which had splendid beds set in alcoves at one end, were the rooms where the occupants received their guests; and the closets, or *cabinets*, beyond these were used for intimate meetings or private business.

It was a modified version of this plan, with servants' rooms but no antechambers, which Roger Pratt had introduced at Coleshill before Vaux-le-Vicomte was designed, and in effect its adoption in England involved little more than changing the names and uses of rooms. By the end of the century, central great chambers were known as *salons* or saloons, withdrawing chambers had become more public and were being used as waiting rooms, and in some houses ante-

67. Chatsworth House, Derbyshire, 1686. The four great rooms and two small rooms which comprise the state apartment are on the second floor. This may be a survival from the original house, which was begun in 1549 by Bess of Hardwick, who later used the same arrangement at Hardwick Hall. But it is also possible that her descendant, the first Duke of Devonshire, followed her example when he remodelled it. In any event this great suite of rooms rivals Hardwick for impressive grandeur.

Wren's contribution as a designer of private houses may have been minimal, but since he fostered a team, or more accurately a school, of craftsmen to work on his great public and royal buildings, his indirect influence can be seen in all the great houses of the late seventeenth and early eighteenth centuries. Although the ceiling in the state bedroom at Chatsworth was painted by a Frenchman, Louis Laguerre, who had been trained at Versailles, the carved and inlaid panelling was the work of Samuel Watson and other craftsmen who were working under the direction of William Talman.

chambers had even been built between the saloons and the withdrawing chambers. French names were also used for some of the servants: the yeoman of the bedchamber, for example, became the *valet de chambre*.

A visitor to a house could judge his estimate in the eyes of its master by the extent to which he progressed through his host's apartment. The withdrawing chamber was now the room to which all the guests retired after dinner in the saloon, and in houses where there was no antechamber it was also the room where the master met his tenants and anyone else who called on minor business. Chosen guests were received in the bed-chamber, and the greatest compliment of all was to be invited into the closet, or cabinet. It was Charles II who introduced the custom of receiving his ministers of state in the cabinet of the royal apartment at Whitehall.

68. The south front of Chatsworth. William Talman was the first architect to work on the rebuilding of Chatsworth and his great design for the south front, which contains the state apartment, represents a complete break with the earlier tradition of high-pitched roofs and restrained and even minimal architectural detail. At the time Chatsworth was being rebuilt, the sash window made its appearance, possibly from Holland, and it was immediately incorporated into the design by Talman.

There were, however, two differences in the English version of the plan. In the first place the English houses still had a parlour for family meals, although a few of the builders of new houses retained the symmetry of their plan by moving it down from the ground floor to the basement. In the second place, despite the fact that the English adopted all the French formality by day, they did not at first adopt it by night as well. English husbands and wives shared the same bed every night, whereas the French had separate matching *appartements* on either side of the *grand salon*. As a result, the English hosts had a set of rooms as splendid as their own which could be used by their most honoured guests, and additional rooms were built beside the bedchambers which the husbands used as dressing-rooms. This arrangement was found to be so convenient that, in the early eighteenth century, when the English succumbed to the French custom and parted for the night, the new houses were still built with dressing-rooms.

One of the first houses to be built in accordance with the French plan was Ragley Hall in Warwickshire, which was designed by Robert Hooke for Charles II's Secretary of State, Lord Conway. By the time Ragley was begun, around 1679, Baroque interiors had become the height of fashion – Inigo Jones himself had used Baroque motifs in the double-cube room at Wilton, and in 1675 Hugh May and the great wood-carver Grinling Gibbons had designed the first totally Baroque interiors at Windsor Castle. But, as at Ragley, the Baroque influence on exteriors was limited to a few decorations around the windows and pediments. In 1686, however, when the fourth Earl of Devonshire began to remodel his Tudor house at Chatsworth in Derbyshire, adapting it to the French plan, he gave it a Baroque exterior as well.

William Cavendish, fourth Earl of Devonshire and a direct descendant of Bess of Hardwick, was one of the leading opponents of James II. When the king sent troops to arrest him, the earl locked the troops up instead; and while Chatsworth was being remodelled, he joined in persuading the House of Lords to invite the king's son-in-law and nephew, William of Orange, to replace him. By the time the work was finished, in 1696, the new King William III had rewarded William Cavendish with a dukedom.

In a Baroque house, each façade differs from the others, and at Chatsworth they were even the work of three separate architects. The south and east fronts are by an unruly architect called William Talman, who was building Uppark in Sussex for Lord Tankerville at the same time and was dismissed from Chatsworth after nine years. The north front is thought to be

70. The west front, Chatsworth. This front stands on Talman's great terrace and was built fifteen years after the south front, by which time Talman had been dismissed by the duke. The architect may have been the duke himself.

69. (*Left*) Uppark, Sussex, 1690. The west front from the dairy. More modest houses like Uppark were designed in the typical post-Restoration style – a style that was eminently suited to manor houses and even farmhouses.

by Thomas Archer, who had recently returned from Italy with such a passion for Baroque that it almost matched Jones's passion for Classicism. The most magnificent, the west front, is probably by the duke himself.

When it was finished, Chatsworth was the most 'modern' house in England. It had at least ten water-closets, with brass fittings, cedarwood cases, marble bowls for the duke and duchess and alabaster bowls for their guests. There was a grotto with a bathroom which had blue and white marble walls, black, white and red marble tiles on the floor and a sunken white marble bath, big enough for two, with hot and cold running water. And in the family parlour there was a large marble buffet, a successor to the laver, with shelves for storing glass and china and basins with taps on either side.

In most houses at this time the water was pumped by hand into high cisterns, from which it was forced by gravity into the lead pipes and taps. But by now it was possible to pump it mechanically. In 1681 Sir Samuel Moreland had introduced a pump at Windsor Castle which was driven by a water wheel; and it was one of these that William Talman installed at Uppark to force the water up a three-hundred-foot hill. At Chatsworth, however, there was no need for pumps. The

water came from the moors high above the house, its own natural pressure was enough to force it into the cisterns, and on the southern front there was a beautiful long canal into which the water cascaded down a flight of steps.

Chatsworth was also one of the earliest houses to be fitted with the new double-hung sash windows, which are thought to have been introduced from Holland. These windows became so popular that they were soon used to replace the rectangular casements on most of the recently built houses, such as Coleshill, and they were to remain a 'hall-mark' of English houses for nearly two hundred years. They were not always so popular with foreign visitors, however. At the end of the nineteenth century the French actress Sarah Bernhardt wrote, 'English windows open only half way, either the top half or the bottom half. One may even have the pleasure of opening them a little at the top and a little at the bottom, but not at all in the middle. The sun can not enter openly, nor the air. The window keeps its selfish and perfidious character. I hate the English windows.'

Since Chatsworth was a remodelling of an older house, it was not possible to fit it to the French plan symmetrically. The great dining chamber, or saloon, was at one end with a single series of state rooms leading off it along the southern front. But there was a large mirror in the opposite wall, which gave the impression of a second apartment when all the doors in the real one were open.

71. Easton Neston, Northamptonshire, 1699. Wren was certainly consulted about this house and may well have built the wings, of which only that on the left remains. The great house itself is the only house designed by Wren's assistant, Nicholas Hawksmoor. Like the south front of Chatsworth, it derives from French rather than Italian houses at a time when Louis XIV's court was proving the most powerful influence in Europe.

There was also one new house in which the plan was not entirely symmetrical. Easton Neston in Northamptonshire, which was begun around 1699, has a large, old-fashioned hall running parallel to the entrance, specially created to accommodate the marbles which its owner, Sir William Fermor, had acquired from the Earl of Arundel's collection. Like Chatsworth, it is a tall, ornate rectangle, and it was the first building to be designed independently by Nicholas Hawksmoor, an architect who had gone down to London from Northamptonshire twenty years earlier to work as a domestic clerk for Sir Christopher Wren, and had risen within a few years to be his principal assistant.

A more typical Baroque house of this period is Chicheley House in Buckinghamshire, which has been attributed to both Thomas Archer and Francis Smith. The façades are much less elaborate than those at Chatsworth and Easton Neston, but even these two houses are restrained by the standards of their

72. Chicheley House, Buckinghamshire, 1713–19. The breaking of the strict Classical rules that was perpetrated by Baroque architects often achieved slightly bizarre results when adopted for smaller houses. The Baroque style was designed to impress and overawe, and when used on great houses like Chatsworth, both in the architecture of the exterior and the decoration of the interior, the sheer scale of the building carries the dramatic weight and impact of the design. Chicheley has been attributed to at least two architects, but whoever was responsible has not quite succeeded in his desire to impress, achieving only a delightful eccentricity.

73. Castle Howard, Yorkshire, 1699. Vanbrugh's domed hall brings the drama and movement of the exterior inside the house. The projection and recession of the wall surfaces, with the eye constantly being led through arches to further spaces, produces exactly that effect of awe which was intended. Although most of the craftsmen employed at Castle Howard were English, the painting in the hall was executed by the Italian Pellegrini and the great niche was the work of Italian plasterers.

74. Vanbrugh's great design for Castle Howard was never accomplished in its entirety. Had it been, it would have outshone even Blenheim.

European contemporaries. While Hawksmoor was designing Easton Neston, however, the First Lord of the Treasury, Charles Howard, Earl of Carlisle, was preparing to build a huge flamboyant house in Yorkshire which was to be entirely in the Baroque spirit. He had originally commissioned William Talman to design it, but they had quarrelled over costs and instead he had offered the job to a friend who had never designed anything before. To make up for the new architect's inexperience, Wren suggested that Hawksmoor should be invited to act as his assistant. Hawksmoor deserved better: after his long association with Wren, he was at last proving his own very considerable talent. But he was so modest and loyal to Wren that he accepted. He left Easton Neston to work on the new house, Castle Howard, and began another long association with the new architect, John Vanbrugh.

Vanbrugh was the grandson of a Protestant refugee from Flanders. In 1686, at the age of 22, he was commissioned in the Earl of Huntingdon's Regiment of Foot, but he resigned soon afterwards when he discovered that he was about to be posted

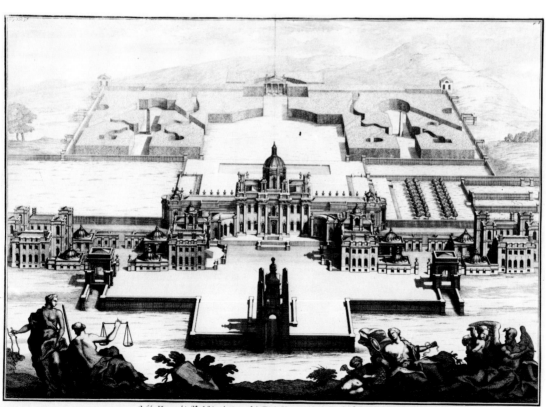

Castle Howard in Yorkshire the Seat of the Right Honourable the Earl of Carlisle &c

C. Campbell Delin.   H. Hulsbergh Sculp.

to tedious garrison duty in Guernsey. After that he went to France, and in 1690, after Louis XIV had declared war on England, he was arrested in mysterious circumstances. A woman in Paris had apparently denounced him for leaving the city without an enemy alien's passport, and when the French authorities found him he was sketching their fortifications at Calais. The French imprisoned him there as a spy and then transferred him to the Bastille, where he passed the time writing the first draft of a play, *The Provok'd Wife*. Two years later, when he was equally mysteriously released, he returned to England and joined the marines. But after another two years he resigned again and turned to playwrighting instead. For the rest of his life he delighted in his reputation as Captain Vanbrugh who had fought in the recent wars against France, and even today he is often referred to as having started his career as a distinguished soldier, whereas in fact he never saw a day's action in his life.

On Boxing Day 1696, *The Relapse by Captain Vanbrugh* opened at Drury Lane to universal acclaim, and five months later a revised version of *The Provok'd Wife* began a run that was to be even more successful. Within two or three years, Vanbrugh was established as one of the outstanding playwrights of his generation, second only to William Congreve. And then, in 1699, his friend Lord Carlisle invited him to design Castle Howard and he accepted, to the astonishment of everyone, including Jonathan Swift:

> *Van's genius, without thought or lecture,*
> *Is hugely turned to architecture.*

Vanbrugh became the leading exponent of Baroque architecture in England. But he was much more of a Classicist than his European contemporaries: his vast theatrical houses had a Palladian symmetry, and he created his effects with scale and the juxtaposition of massive blocks rather than lavish decorative details. Architectural historians have always argued, however, about the extent of his debt to the self-effacing genius of Nicholas Hawksmoor. Perhaps Sir John Summerson had the best answer: 'It is that to Vanbrugh we chiefly owe the daring novelties of composition which are the outstanding characteristics of the houses . . . but it was Hawksmoor who discovered (had, indeed, already discovered) the mode of expression appropriate to these adventures.' Or perhaps the layman can judge for himself by looking at the houses they designed together, such as Castle Howard and Blenheim Palace, and comparing them with the houses each designed alone, such as Hawksmoor's Easton Neston and Vanbrugh's

Seaton Delaval in Northumberland.

At Castle Howard the massive central block contains an enormous hall in the shape of a Greek cross rising through two storeys to a tall dome, and on the exterior its height is accentuated by gigantic pairs of Doric pilasters and by the long, low, twisting wings that flank it. The main building was completed in 1712, but Hawksmoor returned after Vanbrugh's death in 1726 to build the Temple of the Four Winds and a mausoleum for the Earl of Carlisle. Horace Walpole, the author and son of England's first Prime Minister, visited the house over fifty years later: 'I was infinitely struck and surprised by the first view of Castle Howard from the new road, which is like a Terrass opposite to it. The ingredients compose the grandest scene of real magnificence I ever saw. . . . The house, tho' the style is bad, is far superior to Blenheim and has little of its ponderosity.'

It was while they were building Castle Howard that Vanbrugh and Hawksmoor were invited to build Blenheim Palace for John Churchill, first Duke of Marlborough, apparently as a result of a meeting between Vanbrugh and the duke at the theatre. The house was to be the gift of a grateful nation to the hero who had defeated the French, and it was designed as a massive monument to his glory, but the story of its building was more like the theme from one of Vanbrugh's comedies.

The first act opened with Queen Anne approving Vanbrugh's designs, despite the reservations of the beautiful but ill-tempered duchess, who had been her close friend since childhood. But in the same year as the work began, 1705, the duchess fell from favour with the queen; and after a general election of 1710 had brought the duke's Tory opponents to power, the queen supported her ministers in ordering the treasury to cease payments for Blenheim. When the workmen turned to the duke for their wages, the duke, with some justification, saw no reason why he should pay for his own reward. By 1712 the work had come to a halt. The duke and duchess departed to live abroad, and Vanbrugh and Hawksmoor went off to work together on other houses.

At the opening of the second act, after the accession of George I, the Marlboroughs were restored to favour and Vanbrugh was knighted. In the summer of 1716, at the expense of the Treasury, work began again at Blenheim. But the duchess and her architect quarrelled incessantly, and in November Vanbrugh walked out on her, ending his last angry letter with, 'You have your way, Madam, for I will never trouble you more unless the Duke of Marlborough recovers so far, to shelter me from such intolerable treatment.' Many

Engrav'd for the Universal Magazine for I. Hinton in Newgate Street

Blenheim House

75. Blenheim Palace, Oxford-shire, 1705–24. The individual contributions of Vanbrugh and Hawksmoor to Castle Howard and Blenheim are virtually impossible to disentangle, but Blenheim may give a clue. Seen from a great distance across the park, the whole composition is magnificently theatrical, resembling a town rather than a house, and in all his houses Vanbrugh produced such theatrical effects. Closer to, the component parts seem heavy and never quite coordinated. But if smaller sections are isolated to the point where they can be studied without distraction, the mastery of detail is magnificent and must surely be due to Hawksmoor.

76. The most famous French and English mural painters both worked at Blenheim. Laguerre, who worked in a number of great houses, including Chatsworth, painted the saloon.

years later the duchess wrote to a friend, 'I have always had the misfortune to suffer very great mischiefs from the assistance of architects.'

The third act was poignant farce. Since the duke was sick, work continued under the supervision of the duchess, with the assistance of her cabinetmaker, James Moor. But payments from the Treasury were slow. In 1720 the masons sued the duke for the arrears of their wages and won; and in the following year the furious duchess sued almost everyone for conspiracy 'to load the Duke of Marlborough with the pay-ment of debts due' and for 'charging excessive and unreason-able rates'. In 1722, however, when the responsibilities of the house became too much for her, she turned for help to Nicholas Hawksmoor, who was now designing beautiful churches in London. In spite of the fact that he was one of the people she was suing, the good-natured Hawksmoor agreed to return to Blenheim to supervise its completion. When Vanbrugh came to see the finished building in 1725, a year before his death, he was not even allowed into the grounds.

Blenheim is the only house in England large enough to rival the palace of Versailles. Internally it is a huge extension of the French plan: the hall leads to a saloon with magnificent state apartments on either side of it, and on the east front, matching the 180-foot gallery on the west, there is a central dining

chamber flanked by private apartments for the duke and duchess. Although he meant the house to be a monument, Vanbrugh also designed it to be functional. In the face of criticism, he protested that his houses were the most convenient ever planned. But to most people, even at the time, Blenheim was ostentatious and impractical. When the great French dramatist and philosopher Voltaire saw it, he said, 'What a great heap of stone without charm or taste.' The Duchess of Marlborough, inevitably, called it 'a wild, unmerciful house', and Jonathan Swift, equally inevitably, committed his opinion to verse:

> *See, here's the grand approach,*
> *That way is for his grace's coach;*
> *There lies the bridge, and there the clock,*
> *Observe the lion and the cock;*
> *The spacious court, the colonnade,*
> *And mind how wide the hall is made;*
> *The chimneys are so well designed,*
> *They never smoke in any wind:*
> *The galleries contrived for walking,*
> *The windows to retire and talk in;*
> *The council-chamber to debate,*
> *And all the rest are rooms of state.*
> *'Thanks, sir,' cried I, ' 'tis very fine,*
> *But where d'ye sleep, or where d'ye dine?*
> *I find by all you have been telling,*
> *That 'tis a house, but not a dwelling.'*

Most of the great Baroque houses had extensive formal gardens, and many, like Castle Howard and Blenheim, were set in the middle of huge parks. It was wasteful of good farm land, but at the end of the seventeenth century estates were growing larger and more profitable. The process of 'Enclosures' had begun: freeholders were taking over common land and paying scant compensation to the villagers who had used it; and they were soon farming it so much more effectively that they were able to override any opposition with the support of private Acts of Parliament. The lesser gentry, ruined by the 20 per cent land tax which had been levied to pay for the war against France, and only now distinguishable from yeomen by a coat of arms and a few extra hounds, were selling out to richer neighbours, or to merchants. Although the City of London could often provide better returns on investments than did land, the ownership of land was still the only road to social and political recognition, and the merchants were buying as much as always.

77. The ceiling of the entrance hall at Blenheim was the work of Thornhill, who had painted the great hall at Wren's Greenwich Hospital.

Despite the decline of the lesser gentry, however, the richer gentry, doctors, lawyers and the new land-owning merchants were also building houses or improving old ones. Some incorporated Baroque features, which were often applied as clumsily and ignorantly as the Classical features on some early Tudor buildings, but the Baroque style was never typical of English houses. In the first half of the seventeenth century the houses of the gentry and middle classes had mostly been built in the Elizabethan tradition, and since then they had been modelled on houses like Eltham. During the reign of William and Mary they had already evolved into the Anglo-Dutch style that was later to be known as 'Queen Anne'.

The rule for these houses was that they should be 'simple in elegance'. The only traces of Baroque were in the occasional high relief plaster ceilings and the shell-shaped canopies that sometimes replaced triangular or carved pediments over the doors. Built as rectangles or squares, they had two floors of equal height and rows of rectangular sash windows with thick wooden glazing bars; and where there was a third floor, following the example of Sir Roger Pratt, they had dormer windows in the roof so as not to spoil the Classical proportions of their plain brick or stone façades. They were all two rooms

78. Lillingston Dayrell Manor House, Buckinghamshire, the east prospect. This is a seventeenth-century house, pulled down in 1767, remarkable for its mixture of windows, showing casement, mullion and transom and a very early pair of French windows.

The East Prospect of the Manor House of Lillingston Dayrell

The South West Prospect of the Parsonage of Hambleden, Bucks. 1752.

79. The Parsonage, Hambleden, Buckinghamshire, built in 1724. The Baroque technique of applying giant columns or pilasters to the façades of houses has been adopted on this house. The arcading that Vanbrugh used for houses like Seaton Delaval is here carried out in topiary.

thick, even the little square houses having pairs of rooms on either side of the central stair well and entrance hall. In the smaller houses the principal rooms were now on the ground floor, and many, like the beautiful Nether Lypiatt Manor in Gloucestershire, had back stairs and two sets of apartments on the first floor, with closets and servants' rooms on one side of the bedchambers and rooms on the other side that could be used as antechambers or dressing-rooms. Compact and yet spacious enough to be dignified, the plan was so practical and comfortable that it is still being used on modern houses.

In quite a few of these houses, imported pine was used for the timbers instead of expensive home-grown oak; and for the first time the joists were laid with their narrow edges upwards to give the floor-boards greater support. In some, the pine even replaced oak in the panels, which were now much larger and thinner than they had been in earlier houses; and oak also gave way to walnut as the most popular material for the new elegantly curving furniture.

None of the Baroque or Dutch features found their way into cottages. Although many cottages were larger, they were still being built in the traditional styles. In the stone building areas

they became sturdier with bigger windows, and in the rich
sheep-farming Cotswolds, where the builders developed dis-
tinctive dormers in the lofts by creating gables over the front
walls, the limestone cottages with tiled roofs were as well built
and comfortable as early medieval manor houses. But the
thatched and half-timbered cottages were much less well built:
the shortage and price of home-grown timber forced the
carpenters to use misshapen and irregular beams, and they no
longer made any effort to create patterns.

Beside these larger cottages, however, the number of hovels
increased with enclosures. The landless and unemployed poor
began to wander from parish to parish in search of a piece of
common land on which they could scrape a living for their
families, and when they found it, despite efforts to prevent
them, they built the same wretched huts that had been seen in
England for a dozen centuries.

80. Nether Lypiatt Manor,
Gloucestershire, *c.* 1705. This
delightful small manor house is
a perfect example of the
persistence of the post-
Restoration style.

Sir John Vanbrugh designed several great houses after he walked out on the Duchess of Marlborough, including Seaton Delaval, which he designed for Admiral Delaval in 1718. But by then most patrons had lost their taste for extravagant Baroque exteriors. A new Palladian movement was about to begin. In 1713 the Italian architect Giacomo Leoni, who was soon to be one of the instigators of the new movement, had designed Clandon Park in Surrey: it was a Baroque house with four differing façades, but it was as restrained as Chicheley had been over twenty years before, its proportions were Palladian, and when it was finished it had a Palladian interior. And in 1715 the other instigator of the new movement, a Scots architect called Colen Campbell, had designed the totally Palladian Wanstead Hall in Essex.

The Baroque influence on English architecture was fading fast; and it was to end its days as it began, as a sumptuous style

81. Seaton Delaval, Northumberland, 1718. Vanbrugh's smallest country house and one which he designed without the assistance of Hawksmoor. A fire gutted the interior but fortunately the strange and haunting shell has been preserved. The pairs of columns that define the extent of the great hall inside are massive in scale and sit on great cushions of stone which are echoed in the banded stonework of the arcades that connect the main house to the stable and kitchen wings.

82. Ditchley Park, Oxfordshire, 1720. James Gibbs was the maverick architect of his period. He did produce some notable Baroque buildings, like the Radcliffe Camera in Oxford, but only occasionally designed his houses in a Baroque style and never fully succumbed to the immensely powerful new Palladian movement. Ditchley, his finest house, is a perfect example of his unpretentious and very personal style.

Wansted, the Seat of the Earl of Tilney.

S. Wale delin. T. Simpson Sculp.

83. Wanstead Hall, Essex, 1713. The first great house of the new Palladian revival was designed by Colen Campbell. In its composition it resembles the south front of Castle Howard, but, except for the columns of the great portico, all the pilasters that Vanbrugh used at Castle Howard are absent at Wanstead.

for interior decoration. There were no other architects who were prepared to follow in Vanbrugh's adventurous footsteps. While he was designing Seaton Delaval, James Gibbs, more famous for his churches and university buildings than his houses, was designing Sudbrook Lodge in Surrey in a restrained and idiosyncratic combination of the Classical and Baroque styles. But two years later, when Gibbs designed Ditchley Park in Oxfordshire, the only Baroque features that he gave it were a few decorations and statues on the roof: the façades were austere, and the proportions and the flanking pavilions were Palladian. Even Vanbrugh succumbed. In 1723, three years before his death, he designed Grimsthorpe Castle in Lincolnshire for the Duke of Ancaster and gave it a Palladian garden front. The spirit of Inigo Jones had returned.

84. Grimsthorpe Castle, Lincolnshire, 1722. Vanbrugh's last house. Only his entrance front was completed in the rebuilding of a large, early courtyard house. The whole centre section is taken up by one of his finest rooms – a huge entrance hall with stairs at either end. Apart from this Baroque section, the two projecting towers already show signs of his conversion to the Palladian movement that was just beginning. His unexecuted design for the garden front shows an almost total acceptance of it.

85. (*Above*) Averham Park,
Nottinghamshire, *c.* 1695. Here
a typical post-Restoration
house is almost dwarfed by its
two dependencies. They are
not linked to the house and
may even have been added just
before this picture was painted
in 1719.

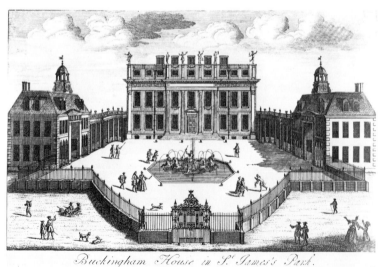

Buckingham House in St James's Park.

CHAPTER 6

The Rule of Taste

86. Buckingham House, London, 1703. In its arrangement of a central block with two dependencies connected by colonnades, this house, designed by William Winde, on the site of what is now Buckingham Palace, had a considerable influence on later houses. Inigo Jones had, of course, produced his own version seventy-four years before at Stoke Park, Northamptonshire, one of his very few private houses.

THE English domestic architecture of the eighteenth century was essentially the architecture of educated aristocrats and gentlemen. For the privileged few it was an age of wealth, confidence and leisure. The century of civil strife was over. Marlborough's victories in Europe had restored the reputation of the British army and left England peaceful, powerful and secure. Scientific curiosity brought rapid improvements in agricultural methods and consequently larger profits from land. The New Learning of the Age of Enlightenment had taught men to question and to doubt. The world which God, 'the Great Mechanic', had created was no longer an unfathomable mystery: its laws, as logical as the Laws of Reason, had only to be investigated to be understood. Nature was romanticised and idealised as a symbol of harmony and order. Men built their houses on high ground with 'commanding prospects' and surrounded them, not with formal gardens, but with 'natural' parks, which were as carefully planned as a landscape painting and decorated with Greek and Roman temples. They looked back to the days of Ancient Rome as the last great age of enlightenment and regarded themselves as its rightful heirs. They learned Latin and Greek at school, they revered the Classical philosophers and authors, they even dressed the statues of their statesmen and soldiers in togas. They visited ancient cities on their Grand Tours and brought back collections of books, drawings, pictures, priceless relics and spurious bargains. Scholarship and patronage of the arts were as fashionable as hunting and dancing. Building houses was a passion. Great patrons and their architects published books of designs; and from these, and from their houses themselves, others followed their examples. In the eighteenth century, as never before, and in England more than in any other country, the great houses set the styles for all the others in towns, countryside and villages.

For gentlemen who aspired to scholarship and taste, a necessary feature of the new house was the library. In the sixteenth century the average gentleman had owned few books: even Lord Burghley, who owned over a thousand, had no room in any of his houses that had been specially designed to contain them. In the first half of the seventeenth century gentlemen kept their books on shelves in their closets. It was not until the second half of that century that rooms known as libraries began to appear: the earliest surviving example, at Ham House in Surrey, was built for the Duke of Lauderdale soon after 1670. But during the eighteenth century every great house of consequence had one, and many of them had studies as well.

Libraries were not sombre places: their books were a source of entertainment as well as instruction. Some families used them as sitting-rooms, and they were open to all the members of the house parties which became larger and larger during the century. The love of learning, literature and the arts did not mean that the English gentleman was dull and studious. On the contrary, he had a boundless zest for living that has rarely been equalled. Although the members of his house parties read books and went on archaeological excursions in the

87. Charles Towneley's library in Park Street, 1781–3, by Johan Zoffany. The painter assembled the finest objects in Towneley's important collection of antique Graeco-Roman sculpture from all over the rest of the house and posed Towneley and three of his friends and fellow collectors amongst them. The room was top-lit from a skylight.

countryside, they also, as always, hunted and shot. They danced in the evenings and sat late into the night over their card-tables and bottles. Gambling was a national disease and the gentry drank as prodigiously as Saxons. Nor were there any separate social 'sets' for sportsmen, politicians or scholars; in Georgian England they were all one 'set'. The great statesmen and men of letters were also the gamblers, dancers and drinkers.

'They tell me that you love a glass of wine,' said George III to his eminent Lord Chancellor, the Earl of Northington.

'Those who have informed Your Majesty have done me great injustice,' said the earl. 'They should have said a bottle.'

Charles James Fox, the great Liberal politician, sometimes gambled for twenty-four hours at a stretch and was said to be capable of losing at a rate of £500 an hour. When a friend called on him one morning after a particularly disastrous night, expecting 'to behold a frantic gamester stretched upon the floor, bewailing his misfortunes,' he found instead that he was reading Herodotus.

Society became much more mobile both literally and metaphorically. The roads improved rapidly: in the first half of the eighteenth century Parliament passed four hundred Road Acts, granting turnpike companies the rights to erect toll bars and charge fees in return for maintaining stretches of highway; and in the second half it passed another sixteen hundred. Carriages became lighter and faster, and by the end of the century they were better sprung, which made them more comfortable and less likely to turn over, although the

88. Design for the library at Holkham by William Kent, *c*. 1735. Today this library is much like Kent's design. Only the decoration of the vaulted cove was omitted, and the cupboards below the bookcases were incorporated into the bookshelves, which are semi-recessed into the walls. It still contains one of the finest private collections of books in the country. The room is white and gold, and with the soft colours of the leather bindings lining the walls, it is one of the most beautiful libraries in any house.

reduction in the number of accidents was not matched by any similar reduction in the numbers of successful highwaymen. The members of what Oliver Goldsmith described as 'polite society' travelled more frequently to each other's houses, sometimes staying for more than a month; they went up to London for 'The Season', and then on to take the waters at one of the fashionable resorts, such as Cheltenham, Scarborough, Buxton and, above all, Bath.

At Bath the aristocracy, gentry and middle classes shared the same baths, pump room and Assembly Room, and under the direction of the great Master of Ceremonies, Beau Nash, they learned to mingle courteously with less inhibiting formality. The son of a Welsh 'gentleman' who owned a share of a Swansea glass-house, Nash earned his living by gambling and performing ridiculous pranks for wagers, such as riding naked through a village on a cow; but he governed Bath like a

89. A party at Wanstead Hall, c. 1730, by William Hogarth. This room in the first great Palladian house shows typical if grand examples of the interior details of these houses. Unlike the ceilings of Baroque houses, such as those in the state rooms at Chatsworth, where the architectural framework is created in paint, the painting here is contained within real architectural details constructed in wood or plaster.

despot, without fear or favour. He laid down strict rules of dress and behaviour: he once pushed a gentleman fully clothed into the bath for using bad language in front of a lady, and one evening he tore the apron off the Duchess of Queensbury, who had presumed to attend an assembly in her morning clothes. If Nash did nothing else with his talents, he at least taught the English manners and style.

The aristocracy were also entertaining the gentry and middle classes more often in their own houses, although the motive was anything but democratic. At a time when only 5 per cent of the population had the vote, large landowners could control several seats in Parliament by extending their patronage to the voting freeholders, finding lucrative jobs for their sons and recognising their sense of their own importance by receiving them as guests at balls and assemblies. But at the same time the gap between the upper and lower classes was widening. Continuing enclosures reduced the common land still further. Broken by competition from the larger and more efficient estates, the yeomen and small freeholders followed the example of the lesser gentry and gave up the unequal struggle. Without these men to employ them or common land to grow food on, many villagers migrated to the towns in search of work, and those who remained provided the cheap labour that paid for the parties and the houses. To Oliver Goldsmith it was an irreparable loss:

> Ill fares the land, to hastening ills a prey,
> Where wealth accumulates and men decay;
> Princes and lords may flourish, or may fade;
> A breath can make them, as a breath has made;
> But a bold peasantry, their country's pride
> When once destroyed, can never be supplied.

The most suitable type of party for the new mixing of the more privileged social classes was the 'assembly', which was defined as 'a stated and general meeting of the polite persons of both sexes, for the sake of conversation, gallantry, news and play'. Like balls, assemblies took place after dinner, which was now served at five o'clock in the evening. By the middle of the century, however, balls and assemblies had merged into one large gathering which was held in several rooms, with guests moving freely from one to the other for dancing, card-playing, supper or just sitting out. In such a world the formal hierarchical progression of state apartments was no longer applicable, and in all but the older houses, which still contained a hall, the need for a room that could be used as a ballroom became increasingly apparent.

During the reigns of the first two Georges, Palladian was the overwhelmingly predominant style for country houses. The seeds of this fashion were sown in 1715 with the publication of two books: the first was an English translation of *The Architecture of A. Palladio in four books, devised, designed and published by Giacomo Leoni*; and the second was the first volume of *Vitruvius Britannicus*, a collection of engravings of country houses with an introduction by Colen Campbell, in which he inveighed against Baroque and called for a return to the 'antique simplicity' of classical architecture. One of the subscribers to the publication of Leoni's book was the Dowager Countess of Burlington, whose 19-year-old son, Richard Boyle, fourth Earl of Burlington, had just returned from his Grand Tour. The earl was one of the most brilliant men of his generation: he was a member of the Privy Council by the time he was 21; and by the time he was 30 he had been elected a Fellow of the Royal Society. As soon as he had read the two books, he was convinced that the time was right for a Palladian movement, and that he was the man to be its founder and leader.

Under the young earl's influence, the fashion for Palladian architecture spread easily among classically educated gentlemen. The 'Rule of Taste' became as immutable as the Laws of Nature. Its arbiters were Burlington and the other great patrons such as the earls of Leicester, Shaftesbury and Pembroke, and its trinity of 'Geniuses', to whom their architects adhered with inhibitingly zealous and punctilious loyalty, were Vitruvius, Palladio and, above all, Jones. In the portrait

90. New Gallery, Somerset House, London, 1661–2. This extension to Somerset House was designed by Inigo Jones but only completed, presumably by his assistant John Webb, ten years after his death. When the members of the now all-powerful Whig aristocracy and their architects turned away in disgust from what they considered to be the excesses of the Baroque, they looked not only to Palladio's buildings but even more to their own countryman Inigo Jones's interpretation of Palladian and Roman architecture. Jones's masterpieces, like the Somerset House gallery and the Banqueting House, were all included in the first volume of Colen Campbell's *Vitruvius Britannicus* along with Vanbrugh's great houses. But this first volume was published in 1715, before the new Palladian and Jonesian revival had established itself as an autocratic Rule of Taste.

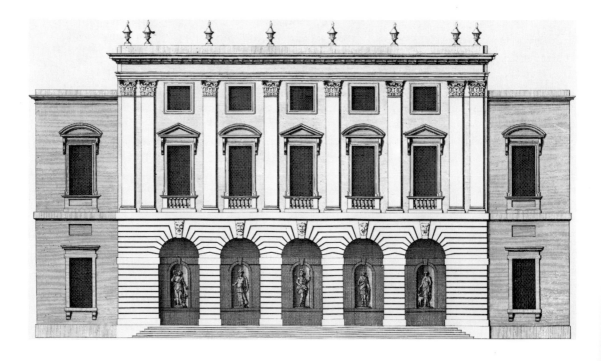

of Lord Burlington by Knapton which now hangs at Chatsworth, the bust of Inigo Jones stands behind him in the shadows.

In 1717 Burlington paid for the publication of the second volume of *Vitruvius Britannicus* and commissioned its author to replace James Gibbs on the rebuilding of Burlington House in Piccadilly. Two years later he returned to Italy to study the architecture of Palladio. While he was there he sought out a young man called William Kent whom he had met in Rome on his Grand Tour. Kent had been trained as a humble coach-decorator in Hull, but in 1709, at the expense of a patron, he and William Talman's son John had set out for Italy to study painting; and he had been living there ever since, earning his keep by showing English tourists round Rome. When Burlington came back to England, Kent came with him to decorate the interiors of Burlington House, and he remained in the earl's household for the rest of his life.

Burlington House has been greatly altered, but Colen Campbell's next great house has not. In 1721 he designed Houghton Hall in Norfolk for England's first Prime Minister, Sir Robert Walpole. It was built under the direction of a local architect, Thomas Ripley, and was not completed until 1735, six years after Campbell's death, by which time James Gibbs had been engaged to give it a Baroque roof with domes at each corner. Beneath that roof, however, the house is pure Palladian; the central block is rectangular and perfectly proportioned, with a pediment and pilasters in the middle and Venetian windows in the shallow corner projections; and there are colonnades connecting it to pavilions on either side.

Like the other great houses of this period, Houghton was built on a low ground floor, which was now known as a 'rustic' and contained several informal family rooms, including a breakfast-room, a coffee-room, a supping parlour and a hunting hall. The kitchens and laundry were in the pavilions, with the servants' rooms above them, and the guests' apartments, which simply consisted of bedrooms and dressing-rooms, were on the top floor of the central block. In some houses the rustic also contained bedrooms, but at Houghton Sir Robert and Lady Walpole's apartments were on the floor above, the Piano Nobili, which also contained the saloon, the library and the state apartments. The interior decorations of these rooms are by both Campbell and William Kent, who also designed the magnificent gold furniture, but only the library and the state drawing-room are Palladian; the others, either by Kent or under his influence, are all exuberantly Baroque.

91. Burlington House, London, *c.* 1717. The most powerful patron and proponent of the new phase of Classical architecture in England was the Earl of Burlington, who employed Campbell to alter his London house. All the emphasis here has been placed on the first floor or piano nobili, and the ground floor has been treated as a base by the use of rusticated stonework, where the joints have been emphasised by deep chamfering at the edges, producing a strong foundation-like quality to support the important architectural treatment of the floor above.

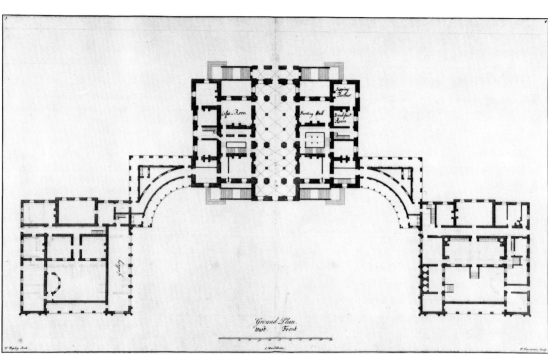

Ground Plan.
West Front

92. Houghton Hall, Norfolk, 1722–35. Colen Campbell's original design was based on Wilton House, with four towers with pediments at each corner. During the course of building, however, James Gibbs was commissioned to substitute domes for the towers.

(*Opposite, below*) The ground floor or rustic, named after the rusticated stonework which faced it, was, as the plan shows, used by the family for everyday living, and the whole of the piano nobili was taken up by the state apartments. Even before the house was finished, the rooms in these apartments, each with a bedchamber and a withdrawing-chamber, had begun to be used for general entertaining, although the owner's apartment was retained, as well as one state bedchamber with its magnificent bed designed by William Kent.

(*Above, left*) William Kent was called in to decorate and design furniture for a number of the rooms. This drawing shows his proposed treatment for one end of the saloon.

(*Left*) The plan for the first floor.

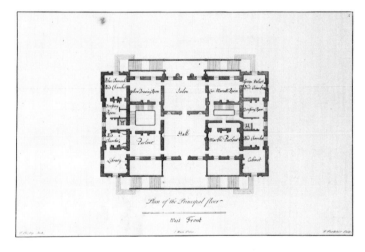

Plan of the Principal floor

West Front

Houghton was originally designed with a symmetrical French plan, but it took so long to build that by the time it was completed the changing social habits had made the plan obsolete. Walpole used it while the builders were still working on it. He held regular 'congresses' for his political colleagues and the local gentry, at which, according to one guest, Lord Hervey, they were 'up to the chin in beef, venison, geese, turkeys, etc., and generally over the chin in claret, strong beer and punch'. In 1731 Walpole received a visit from the Duke of Lorraine, during which he spent an extravagant £15 a night on lighting the cubed stone hall with 130 candles and the saloon with another 50. There were so many guests on that occasion that they had to dine in the hall, which is probably why, shortly afterwards, he decided to destroy the symmetry of the plan and instructed Kent to decorate one of the withdrawing chambers as a state dining-room.

Campbell's next house after Houghton was Mereworth Castle in Kent, which he designed in 1723 for Colonel the Hon. John Fane, later Earl of Westmorland. It was an experiment which both he and Burlington had been considering for some time: a pure reproduction of a Palladian villa. Burlington, who had already designed Tottenham Park in Wiltshire for his brother-in-law and a dormitory for his old school, Westminster, was eager to design a villa of his own, but he was happy to learn by watching Campbell try the idea out on someone else first. Mereworth's only similarity to a 'castle' was the fact that it was surrounded by a moat; the house itself, intended as a country retreat, was copied from the Villa Capra at Vicenza, also known as La Rotonda, which Palladio had designed for the same purpose. There are, however, differences between Mereworth and the Villa Capra: at Mereworth only two of the four porticos have steps leading up to them, and the dome above the central hall is much larger. Unlike an Italian villa, the English version had to have fireplaces in every room, which might have meant that its roofline was broken by chimneys. Campbell's ingenious solution was to make the dome larger and to build twenty-four flues inside it which run up from the fireplaces to the lantern on top of it.

When Burlington designed his own villa at Chiswick two years later, he accepted that it was an English house and gave it little chimneys, although he managed to retain his Classical theme by designing them in the shape of obelisks. Burlington's villa is a much less faithful reproduction of the Villa Capra. It is as much Roman as Palladian, the windows in the octagonal dome are copied from Roman baths, and instead of

93. The hall at Houghton, a single cube of 40 feet, remains much as Campbell designed it, although the plasterwork was added to the ceiling cove.

being symmetrical it has only two porticos, with elaborate stairs on either side of them. On the entrance front, beside the stairs, there are two statues in Roman togas – Andrea Palladio and Inigo Jones. Burlington did not design the house to be lived in; it was used only for entertaining and for housing his art collection, and the influence of Inigo Jones is apparent in the appropriately magnificent interiors, which, like the gardens, were designed by William Kent, who had just finished editing Jones's drawings.

One of the frequent visitors at Chiswick was Burlington's friend Thomas Coke, Earl of Leicester, who had by coincidence met William Kent in Naples on his own first Grand Tour and had travelled north with him through Rome. They were an unlikely trio, the reserved and scholarly Burlington, the hedonistic Leicester and the ill-educated, charming and emotional Kent, who went to the opera twice a week to think himself 'out of this Gothick counterey'. But they had one thing in common: a passion for architecture. Together they designed a new house for Leicester's estate at Holkham, in Norfolk, which was to be even grander than

94. Chiswick House, London, 1725. One whole side of Chiswick is taken up with a gallery divided into three sections. At one end of the centre section is an octagonal room and at the other a circular room. The only colours used throughout the three spaces were white and gold.

95. Lord Burlington designed Chiswick as a version of Palladio's Villa Capra for himself – not to live in but to use for entertaining in and housing his collection of pictures and, on the ground floor, his library. The decoration of the interior was entrusted to William Kent, by now firmly established in Lord Burlington's household.

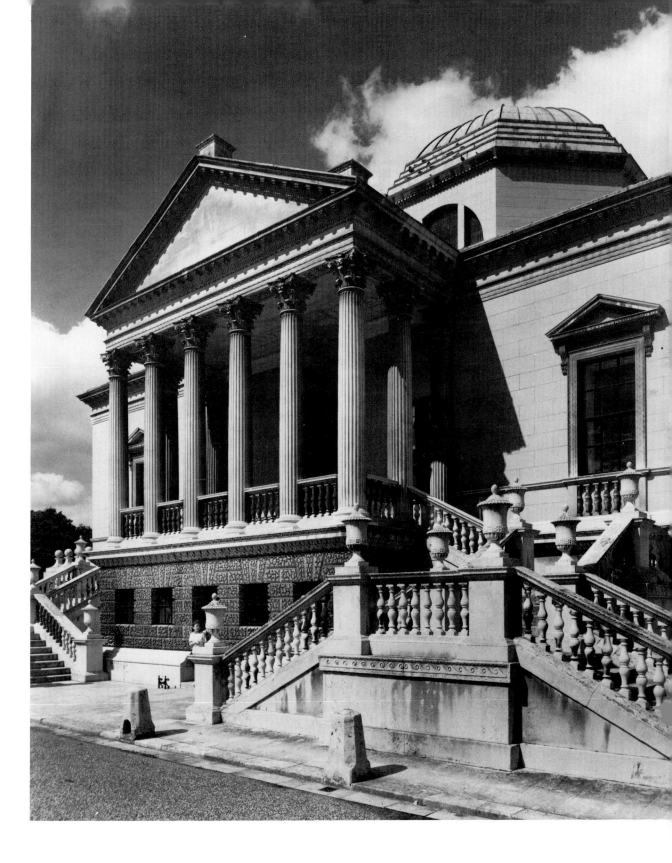

nearby Houghton. Begun in 1734, it took thirty years to build, and by the time it was finished, Kent, Burlington and Leicester were dead.

Although Kent wanted to build Holkham in Bath stone, Leicester overruled him, since, apart from being anxious to save money where he could, he was eager to make it as Classical as possible by using brick. He even had the bricks made on the estate and copied from a piece of Roman brick which he had brought back with him from Italy. Based on Palladio's Villa Moncenigo and set in a park designed by Kent, Holkham has a central block with four flanking pavilions containing the chapel, the libraries, the kitchens and a guest wing. Under the influence of Leicester and Burlington, the façades are much more austere than they were in Kent's original plans, and after they were built they acquired an added austerity when the gilded glazing bars, which are now being replaced, fell victim to the Victorian predeliction for plate glass. The interior, however, is everything that Kent intended. Inside the simple front door, in the rustic, there is one of the most beautiful and ornate halls in England. The steps at one end rise to the saloon through a colonnade that was copied from one of Palladio's churches; the designs of the frieze and the coffered panels in the roof were derived from those in Roman temples, and the deep flowered ribs in the ceiling were taken from a drawing by Inigo Jones.

Kent was one of the very few great architects who could turn his hand with equal genius to designing interiors, furniture or landscapes. He designed furniture not only for his own interiors but also for Chatsworth and Wilton, and at Holkham and Stowe in Buckinghamshire he pioneered the English style of informal landscaping which was soon to reach its zenith in the work of Lancelot 'Capability' Brown. As Horace Walpole wrote:

> His oracle was so much consulted by all who affected taste, that nothing was thought compleat without his assistance. He was not only consulted for furniture, as frames for pictures, glasses, tables, chairs etc., but for plate, for a barge, or a cradle. And so impetuous was fashion, that two great ladies prevailed upon him to make designs for their birth-day gowns.

96. Mereworth Castle, Kent, 1723. In all, four variations of Palladio's Villa Capra at Vicenza were built in England, although numerous architects made designs on the same theme. Campbell's version is the nearest to the original (Palladio's design having a similar dome to Mereworth). Two later versions were demolished. All four were planned around a domed rotunda.

In his effort to spread the influence of Palladian architecture, Burlington arranged for Kent's appointment as Deputy Surveyor of the Board of Works, where he designed his most famous building, the Horseguards in Whitehall; and he also secured a position in the Board of Works for another of his

proteges, Henry Flitcroft, a former carpenter who designed the enormous sprawling Wentworth Woodhouse in Yorkshire. But the Palladian influence spread equally through the work of other architects to whom Burlington was not a patron, and two of the most eminent, Sir Robert Taylor and James Paine, were among the earliest to take on articled pupils in their London offices and to train them in their own style.

Taylor's first country house was Harleyford Manor in Buckinghamshire, which he designed around 1755. Although it was a compact house, it was intended as much for entertaining as for family living, and as such it was the first house to abandon the formality of the French plan. There was no saloon; the only apartments were the bedrooms and dressing-rooms on the first floor. On the ground floor a vestibule led to a central hall with a staircase which had a drawing-room beyond it and a library and a dining-room on either side. Apart from having doors which opened onto the hall or the vestibule, the three rooms were also interconnected: when servants came up from the kitchen in the basement, they could reach any room without going through one of the others; and when the family gave a ball, the whole house could act as a circular apartment, with the guests moving round it and across the hall and the vestibule for dancing in the drawing-room, cards in the library and supper in the dining-room.

97. Holkham Hall, Norfolk, 1734. Designed by its owner Lord Leicester, Lord Burlington and William Kent, Holkham is one of the largest of Palladian houses. Its exterior suffers from Lord Leicester's insistence that it should be built of brick and not stone as Kent had suggested. The whole central block was one vast area for entertainment and the display of Lord Leicester's collection of magnificent sculpture and pictures. Joined to this great central pile are four substantial dependencies for the kitchens, chapel, library and guests respectively.

98. Kent's great *tour de force* at Holkham is the entrance hall. The gigantic space uses the full height of the house, and the great flight of steps, occupying the apse opposite the front door, leads from ground level to the piano nobili, which at Holkham is indeed noble.

100. Section of a London house by John Yenn, 1774. By the time Holkham was finished, in 1764, the first great interiors of Robert Adam and William Chambers in the newly fashionable neo-Classical taste had begun to appear. The rigidly formal pattern of living had long since passed, and with it the seemingly endless vistas through room after room. By the mid-1750s houses were being planned around a central staircase which gave access to all the rooms, as in this house by John Yenn, who was working in the office of William Chambers. Chambers was the first architect to produce this type of drawing, which gave not only the outline of the decoration but also the colour scheme.

99. (*Left*) Wardour Castle, Wiltshire, *c.* 1770. The great central staircase is decorated by James Paine in the neo-Classical taste.

This principle, which may have been suggested by the central hall in a Palladian villa, was also used in town houses; and in 1769 James Paine applied it at a much larger house, Wardour Castle, which he designed for the Earl of Arundel. Like all the other great houses of the time, Wardour still had a saloon, although saloons were now being used for little more than dancing and receiving guests, and the most important room in most new houses was an elegantly decorated dining-room. But at Wardour the apartments on either side of it were laid out around a colonnaded and circular staircase hall which rose through the centre of the house and was lit from above, like the hall at Harleyford.

By the time Wardour was designed, however, other great houses, such as Hagley Hall in Worcestershire, were being built with versatile plans in which a variety of rooms could be incorporated in 'circuits' of different sizes, depending on the number of guests. Hagley was designed around 1752 for Lord Lyttleton, a Privy Councillor, by a local architect, Sanderson Miller. Externally it is a tall stone copy of the central block at Holkham without its portico, but internally it is completely different. A main hall leads to the saloon across a corridor which has smaller staircase halls at either end of it. On the left

of the saloon a door leads into a series of private apartments
which run round one of these halls to the library at the front of
the house, and a door on the right leads through a drawing-
room and a gallery round the other hall to a dining-room.
Since the drawing-room and the dining-room open into the
hall between them, it was possible to use these two rooms
with the gallery for a small assembly; for larger gatherings the
hall and the saloon could be included in the 'circuit'; and for a
grand ball the apartments and the library could be opened up,
turning the whole house into one huge 'circuit'.

In his instructions to his architect, Lord Lyttleton specifi-
cially stipulated that the dining-room and drawing-room
should be separated by more than a wall, 'to hinder the ladies

from the noise and talk of the men when left to their bottle, which must sometimes happen, even at Hagley'. Surprisingly, there is no certainty as to why English ladies withdrew after dinner. The custom started at the end of the seventeenth century, at a time when coffee and tea had become fashionable, and in his *Life in the English Country House*, Mark Girouard has suggested that, since these drinks were usually served in the drawing-room and prepared for the guests by the hostess herself, the ladies accompanied her when she went to make tea. It has also been suggested, less convincingly however, that the custom arose when the ladies withdrew discreetly on cold winter evenings to allow the gentlemen to use chamber pots instead of the garden.

101. Hagley Hall, Worcestershire, 1752. Hagley Hall is derived from the central block at Holkham, but here the Palladian exterior hides an interior that is marvellously decorated with Rococo plasterwork.

102. Constable Burton Hall, Yorkshire, 1768. John Carr, or Carr of York as he is frequently referred to, was probably the most prolific of provincial architects. His houses in the Midlands and the north are all in the Palladian tradition. He and James Paine were the greatest of the second-generation Palladian architects and both of them were ready to adapt to current fashions like the Rococo or neo-Classical interiors that their clients demanded, while maintaining propriety in their Palladian exteriors.

Apart from Sanderson Miller, there were many other provincial architects who followed the Rule of Taste and spread its influence among the gentry and merchants. In the north the most eminent was John Carr of York, whose beautiful Constable Burton Hall is a perfect example of the medium-sized Palladian country house. And in the west the most eminent was John Wood the elder of Bath. Together with his son and namesake, John Wood was to achieve immortality by developing Bath into a Palladian city, but he also built the magnificent Prior Park for one of his backers, Ralph Allen. Allen was an assistant postmaster who had managed to marry a general's daughter. While Wood was developing Bath, Allen bought the Combe Down limestone quarries, from which the stone could be shipped down the River Avon to the city, and in 1735 he commissioned Wood to build him a Palladian mansion with pavilions as an advertisement for the quality of his product.

The influence of the Rule of Taste, however, was spread as much by books as by individual architects or examples. Apart from the second volume of *Vitruvius Britannicus*, Burlington also published *Designs of Inigo Jones*, which had been edited by Kent; and James Gibbs published his *Book of Architecture*, in which one of the drawings is said to have inspired the design of the White House in Washington. From these, and in particular from the many more practical pattern books that followed, amateur architects and local craftsmen were able to reproduce the features and shapes of great houses more faithfully than ever before, and one of the beautiful virtues of Palladian architecture was that its principles could be applied with equal harmony to stone palaces, brick terraces, farmhouses and humble little cottages. All over England houses were being built or remodelled with proportion, symmetry, pediments and rectangular windows; and their style, Classical in origin and still copied by developers, is now simply known as 'Georgian'.

CHAPTER 7

Spread of an Ideal

103. Marble Hill, Twickenham, Middlesex, 1728, one of the earliest and most perfect small Palladian houses, was built for George II to give to his mistress. The centre on this side is taken up by a low hall above which is the one large room in the house, the saloon. Its design is accredited to the Earl of Pembroke and Roger Morris. They were also responsible for the Palladian bridge at Wilton which is so appropriately situated in front of the magical garden façade. Although Roger Morris may have done the majority of the drawings, this partnership underlines the level of architectural knowledge that the rich patrons possessed at this period.

THE villas at Mereworth and Chiswick started the fashion for the dozens that were built soon after them along the Thames from Chelsea to Twickenham. Just as the merchant princes of Venice had built villas on the banks of the Brenta, so too the courtiers of London built summer retreats beside the Thames to avoid the heat and stench of the city. Few of these villas have survived in the face of a spreading city and redevelopment, but one of the finest has now been beautifully restored – Marble Hill in Twickenham, presented by George II to his intellectual mistress, the Countess of Suffolk, and designed for her by the Earl of Pembroke and Roger Morris. Like Marble Hill, most of these villas were simpler than Mereworth and Chiswick, and for the merchants, doctors, lawyers and soldiers who sought to follow the Rule of Taste in their own more modest houses, they were an ideal example of the dignified harmony of Palladian architecture.

Many of the leading architects were commissioned to build

104. Ebberston Lodge, Yorkshire, 1718. Colen Campbell's miniature version of a Palladian mansion. Even this tiny house has considerable grandeur. One of the dependencies was demolished.

smaller houses. Colen Campbell designed one house, Ebberston Lodge in Yorkshire, which was so small that it would have fitted into the hall at Houghton. John Wood the elder built several villas, including the enchanting Belcombe Court in Somerset. But the first architect to specialise in smaller houses was Sir Robert Taylor. Taylor's 'villas' were mostly built for merchants, and, unlike the villas of the aristocracy, they were designed to be lived in all the year round. As at his first country house, Harleyford, he designed them around central halls with differing bays on each façade, which added variety to the shapes of the rooms and gave the exterior a grandeur that belied their size. He also set these houses in the middle of little landscaped parks, allowing his clients to feel that they were living in their own miniature version of one of his large country houses, such as Heveningham Hall in Suffolk.

Unfortunately, few of Taylor's small houses have survived, and most of those that have, like Harleyford, are now dilapidated, but there is one, Asgill House near Richmond in

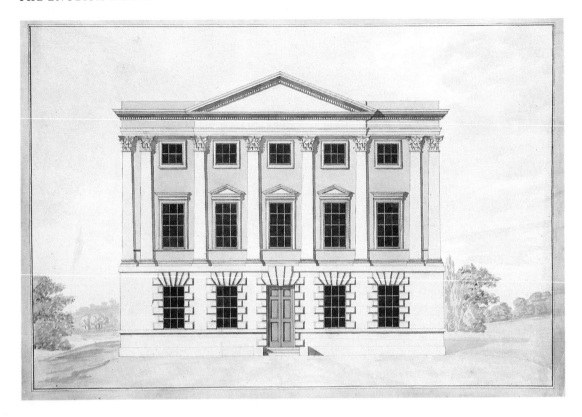

Surrey, which has recently been beautifully restored. Taylor was only the first of many, however. In the second half of the eighteenth century thousands of middle-class villas were built all over England on the outskirts of the cities and spas. As time passed, both they and their grounds became smaller and smaller until, by 1800, the word 'villa' was well on its way to its modern meaning and included almost every genteel suburban residence with any architectural pretensions.

But the demand for small houses was far too great to be met by architects alone. Most of the Georgian houses in England were built, not under the direction of professional architects, but by amateurs and craftsmen who copied them from books. Few of these builders can have owned any of the first handsome and expensive volumes that were published in limited editions by the leading architects and their patrons, and even if they did they could have used them for little more than inspiration and stylistic guidance. There was only one that would have been of any practical assistance. The others dealt solely with large houses and were simply intended to convert their aristocratic readers to the Palladian taste, and perhaps earn a few commissions for the authors – Colen Campbell

106. Asgill House, Richmond, Surrey, c. 1760. Even in this small house, which can never have been more than a weekend cottage on the banks of the Thames, the ground floor is rusticated and the principal rooms are on the first floor. It was designed by Robert Taylor for a rich banker. Taylor was, during the 1750s, the first architect to design comfortable, well-planned villas for the new rich merchant class. Their plans almost invariably had central top-lit staircases and were very compact.

THE
Modern Builder's Assistant;
OR,
A CONCISE EPITOME
Of the Whole
SYSTEM of ARCHITECTURE;
IN WHICH
The various Branches of that excellent Study are eftablifh'd on the moft familiar Principles,
And rendered adequate to every Capacity;
Being ufeful to the Proficient, and eafy to the Learner.

Divided into THREE PARTS.
CONTAINING
I. A Correct View of the FIVE ORDERS, explained in feveral Sheets of Letter-Prefs.
II. Confifting of REGULAR PLANS, ELEVATIONS, and SECTIONS of Houfes, in the moft elegant and convenient Manner, either for the Reception of Noblemen, Gentlemen or Tradefmen with large or fmall Families, adapted to the Tafte of Town or Country.

To which PART is added,
A great Variety of other PLANS for Offices or Out-Houfes adjoining to them of different Dimenfions for Domeftic Ufes;
SUCH AS
KITCHENS, WASH-HOUSES, MALT-HOUSES, BAKE-HOUSES, BREW-HOUSES, DAIRIES, VAULTS, STABLES, COACH-HOUSES, DOG-KENNELS, &c. &c.
Together with the
ESTIMATES of each DESIGN, and Proper INSTRUCTIONS to the WORKMEN how to execute the fame.
III. Exhibiting (ornamental as well as plain) a Variety of CHIMNEY-PIECES, WINDOWS, DOORS, SECTIONS of STAIR-CASES, ROOMS, HALLS, SALOONS, &c. SKREENS for Rooms, alfo CIELINGS, PIERS, and GATE-ROOFS, &c. &c.

The Whole beautifully Engraved on EIGHTY FIVE *Folio Copper Plates*,
From the DESIGNS of
William and *John Halfpenny*, Architects and Carpenters, *Robert Morris*, Surveyor,
AND
T. Lightoler, Carver.

LONDON:
Printed for JAMES RIVINGTON and J. FLETCHER in Pater-nofter Row, and ROBERT SAYER oppofite Fetter-Lane, Fleet-Street.
MDCCLVII.

included all his own work in *Vitruvius Britannicus*, and even William Kent managed to slip in a few of his own designs while editing the *Designs of Inigo Jones*.

The one exception, although still expensive, was the *Book of Architecture* by James Gibbs. Gibbs may have needed to publish a book of his own since he was the only eminent contemporary architect who was not even mentioned in *Vitruvius Britannicus*. Unlike Campbell, he was a Tory, a Catholic and a not entirely convinced Palladian, but it still seems a little petty of Campbell to have excluded his fellow-Scot entirely, particularly after replacing him at Burlington House. Whatever the reason, Gibbs had his revenge when he crowned Campbell's Houghton with a Baroque roof.

Although Campbell had included an illustration of his little Ebberston Lodge in *Vitruvius Britannicus*, Gibbs's *Book of Architecture* was the first important book to contain suggested plans for small and medium-sized houses; and it also contained designs for doors, windows, garden pavilions and many other decorations. In the introduction, Gibbs wrote that the book was intended to 'be of use to such Gentlemen as might be concerned in Building, expecially in the remote parts of the Country, where little or no assistance for Designs can be procured'. In fact it was used further afield than that: several modified versions of his houses were built across the Atlantic in the American colonies. But his influence did not reach 'the remote parts of the country' exactly as he had hoped. By the time his book was published, in 1728, the first of the cheap pattern books had appeared – *Practical Geometry, Applied to the Useful Arts of Building, Surveying, Gardening and Mensuration*, by Batty Langley. Many others followed, and some contained shameless copies of Gibbs's designs for doors and windows.

Batty Langley, the son of a gardener, was not only the first author of a pattern book, he was also the most prolific. Between the publication of his first book in 1726 and his death in 1751, he published at least another twenty of varying merit, including *The Young Builder's Rudiments*, *The Builder's Compleat Assistant*, *The Builder's Jewel* and the almost annual *London Prices of Bricklayers' Materials and Works*. Like Gibbs, Langley presented designs for houses, doors, windows and interior decor, but he also included summaries of building regulations and practical instructions in building techniques and surveying.

After the publication of his first two books, others began to flow onto the market, by Edward Hoppus, Abraham Swann, Robert Morris, William Halfpenny, who was almost as prolific as Langley, T. Lightoler, John Plaw and many more. In

A View of Esher Place in Surry.

109. (*Above*) Esher Place, Surrey, *c.* 1735. Both Vanbrugh and William Kent indulged in playful evocations of medieval architecture. Kent here, like other mid-century architects, imposed strict symmetry on a Gothic building when neither the medieval builders nor the nineteenth-century Gothic imitators would have accepted such an imposition.

107. (*Left, above*) Title page from *The Modern Builder's Assistant,* 1757. Nothing helped the spread of ideas more quickly or efficiently than the pattern books which were being produced in increasing quantities by the middle of the eighteenth century at prices that builders and craftsmen, as well as the minor gentry and clergy, could afford.

108. (*Below*) Design for a fireplace from *The Modern Builder's Assistant.* As this book was published at the height of the vogue for Rococo chinoiserie, it is not surprising that designs like this were included.

1742, Morris, Halfpenny and Lightoler collaborated on *The Modern Builder's Assistant* and soon afterwards they each published books which included plans for farmhouses, barns, stables and garden pavilions. As time passed and tastes changed, the authors published new volumes to cover Gothic and even Chinese architecture. Craftsmen followed their example: in 1733, Francis Price, Surveyor at Salisbury Cathedral, published *The British Carpenter,* which was recommended by James Gibbs and the 82-year-old Nicholas Hawksmoor; and in 1754, the great furniture-maker Thomas Chippendale published *Gentleman and Cabinet-Maker's Director.*

Few of these authors actually built houses, and the only two who built anything worth mentioning were Robert Morris, who had a flourishing practice in Scotland, and John Plaw, whose buildings included the beautiful circular villa of Belleisle on an island in Lake Windermere. Although Langley was a successful landscape gardener and ran a school of architecture in London, where most of his students were carpenters, his own efforts as an architect were widely ridiculed, as indeed were several of his books. When he responded to the popularity of Gothic taste with *Gothic Architecture Restored and Improved by Rules and Proportions,* Horace Walpole remarked furiously that, 'All Langley's books [have] achieved has been to teach carpenters to massacre that venerable species.' Within a few years 'Batty Langley Gothic' had become as much a term of contempt as 'stockbroker Tudor' is today.

With his books selling better than anyone else's, Batty Langley was undeterred, and he was not above criticising the competition himself. In the introduction to *A Sure Guide to Builders*, he wrote:

> The Great Want of Architectural Principles has caused many good-natur'd workmen, such as Halfpenny, Hoar, etc., to communicate what little they knew for the Good of their Fellow-Workmen, in as good a manner as they were capable; but being without Demonstration, they have left Workmen in the dark, and all that they have done, is, therefore, of very little Service; and the Builder's Dictionary (the most surprising, undigested Mess of Medley that yet was ever put together), consists of nothing more than Hearsays, Reports of God knows who, and what, without any real Matters of Fact that either Workman or Master can depend upon.

Batty Langley's books may have been the most widely read, but the best pattern book, which rivalled all Langley's in influence, was *A Complete Body of Architecture* by Isaac Ware. Like Campbell and Kent, Ware published books on the works of other great architects, including his own version of *Designs of Inigo Jones*, and his pattern book, like Gibbs's *Book of Architecture*, was regularly plagiarised by other authors. He went through every stage of construction in greater detail than anyone else. Although he took Palladio as his master, he condemned the English tendency 'to transfer the buildings of Italy right or wrong, suited or unsuited to the purpose, in England', and he warned that 'the art of building cannot be more grand than it is useful; nor its dignity greater praise than its convenience'.

But then Isaac Ware was a practising architect who had trained in Italy. He designed Wrotham Park in Middlesex and several fine houses in London, including the splendid Chesterfield House, which has since been demolished, and his own house, 5 Bloomsbury Square. Since, like Jones and Kent, he was of humble birth, his training has been accounted for in a romantic and almost certainly apocryphal story. According to this story, he was apprenticed to a chimney sweep as a boy, and we are asked to believe that one day he was standing by the basement of the Banqueting House, scratching a drawing of its elevation on the stone, when a fine gentleman came by and was so impressed by his talent that he bought the rest of his term of apprenticeship, educated him and sent him to Italy to study architecture. Needless to say, the story ends with Ware

110. Chesham village, Buckinghamshire, *c.* 1760. Country houses and houses in towns and villages, whether built from scratch or altered and added to like the large house in Chesham village, all show the influence of the Rule of Taste.

111. Butlers Court, Beaconsfield, Buckinghamshire, *c.* 1740.

Elevation of the principal Front of Butler's Court House.

returning a few years later to discover that his patron was none other than Lord Burlington.

Armed with the pattern books of Ware, Langley and the others, amateur architects and local masons and carpenters brought Palladian principles to the provinces. Once the first examples had been set, the aristocratic passion for building seized everyone who could afford it; and many of those who could not remodelled instead. Builders went to ingenious and extrordinary lengths to coerce old asymmetrical houses into some sort of conformity with the Rule of Taste. Exposed timber frames were covered with plaster, brick, brick tiles or even blocks of wood which were then painted to look like stone. Pediments and pilasters were pinned round doors. Wherever the supporting timbers allowed it, windows were relocated at equal intervals; and where they did not, the old, horizontal, rectangular casements could at least be replaced by vertical, rectangular sashes. All over England today, in market towns and villages, there are still hundreds of little Georgian-looking houses with ground floors that are smaller than the upper floors because false walls were built up to their jetties to give them fashionable flush façades.

Except, as always, along the limestone belt, brick became almost universal on all but the humblest of new houses. By the time the eighteenth century was entering its last quarter, brick was often being used instead of timber to support the structure of the house. There was a revival of timber-framing, however, after 1784, when the government imposed a tax on bricks to pay for the Hanoverian and British soldiers who were attempting with notable lack of success to suppress the democratic instincts of the American colonists. Many provincial builders reverted to old techniques, using cob, rubble or cheap bricks between the timbers and facing them with slate, clapboard and tiles, or even brick tiles which could be made to look like real bricks and were not subject to the tax. But by then some of the leading architects were using Liardet's Patent Stucco, which had appeared in 1773 and was the first successful material for rendering brick walls in imitation of stone; and after the appearance of the much more durable and weatherproof Parker's Roman Cement in 1796, the fashion for stucco spread rapidly. Parker's Roman Cement was an excellent product; it was to be used on many of the great Regency terraces, but the speed of its success was due in part to the fact that it came on the market at exactly the right moment – two years earlier, the Government had doubled the brick tax to pay for the rather more successful efforts of the British navy against the French.

112. St John's House, Hoxton, London. This curious house, with its blocked-up windows, may well have been built about the time a window tax was first imposed in 1697. Its eccentric Baroque features certainly indicate that it was once a house of some pretension.

113. Mid-eighteenth-century trade card for wallpaper.

114. Mrs Congreve and her
daughters in their London
drawing-room, 1782. The
speculative builder who was
responsible for building this
typical London house seems to
have skimped on the
architectural detail – the cornice
is noticeably mean. Mrs
Congreve is comfortably off but
not rich – the mahogany
furniture is a trifle old-fashioned
but the pictures and mirrors are
fashionably arranged in pairs.

115. The Corbally family, c. 1775. The wallpaper in this room has been taken down to the skirting and, as was usual at this time, the seat furniture is ranged against the wall and only brought into the middle of the room when in use.

Windows were also subject to tax. The tax was first imposed in 1697 on all houses with more than six windows and was increased several times during the eighteenth century. To save the owners money, while still retaining the symmetry of the façades, many masons built houses with blank windows in the front and rear, which were often painted in black and white to look like glass and glazing bars. At either end they built no windows at all; and since Georgian houses usually had their chimneys inside the walls, creating recesses in the rooms on either side of the projecting chimney breasts, the end walls were completely flat and blank. As a result, many of the houses that were built to this pattern now look as though they are the sole survivors of terraces.

Unlike Queen Anne houses, the Georgian houses often hid their roofs behind parapets. In the early part of the eighteenth century they had brick pilasters on the façades and their doors were surrounded by elaborate classical columns and pediments, but as the century progressed, the façades became simpler, the glazing bars in the windows became thinner and thinner, and by 1800 many houses had doors with no more than little engaged columns in the frame and leaded semi-circular fanlights above.

Internally, however, the plan was very similar to the plan in the Queen Anne houses: square houses had pairs of rooms on either side of a stairwell, and rectangular houses were double

pile. Panelling went out of fashion around the middle of the century. After that the rooms were either painted or wall-papered, and towards the end of the century they were often decorated with delicate Classical plaster-work. Much of the furniture was made out of West Indian mahogany after it had been freed from import duty in 1721. During the reign of George III, however, the timber-merchants imported many other beautiful woods in a variety of grains and shades, and these were used for the inlays and veneering on the loveliest furniture that English craftsmen have ever made.

Imitating the tastes of the rich, the English middle classes collected china and hung pictures and looking glasses on their walls, but their rooms were much less cluttered than they were to become during the following century; and the living-rooms at least were apparently much cleaner than in French houses. The French Duc de la Rochefoucauld, who visited England in the 1780s before he succeeded to his title, recorded with surprise that the English houses were 'constantly washed inside and out, generally on Saturdays'. He was not, however, so impressed by the kitchens: 'The worst thing that could happen to you would be to go into the kitchen before dinner – the dirt is indescribable.'

116. A modest house in Lewes, Sussex, 1787, where the front wall has been built up to form the by now fashionable parapet.

If there were no improvements in kitchen hygiene during the eighteenth century, there were at least a few improvements in the methods of cooking and heating. For most of the century, cooks had to be content with separate cast-iron ovens, which had fires beneath them, and roasting-ranges, which consisted of no more than the kitchen grates with a few trivets above them for hanging pots on and spits in front of them over drip-trays. The cast-iron kitchen grate evolved in the same way as the smaller coal-burning grates in the other rooms. It was free-standing until about 1760; after that it was built-in and had flat tops to the casing at each side, known as hobs, on which pots could be heated. Beside one hob there

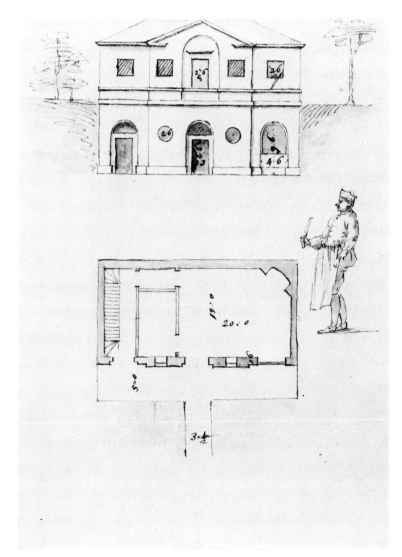

117. Design for a kitchen by William Kent. Even the design of kitchens was affected by the Rule of Taste.

118. The Old Kitchen, St James's Palace. An early-nineteenth-century view of a kitchen which was probably designed by Sir John Vanbrugh in 1717. Improvements made during the late eighteenth century included the addition of top lighting and the installation of cast-iron ovens which were built into the wall.

was a sheet of cast-iron, known as a cheek, which could be moved towards the other hob or away from it, varying the size of the fire between them.

In 1780, however, Thomas Robinson patented an idea so simple that it is astonishing nobody thought of it before. In Robinson's Patent Range, one of the hobs was replaced by an oven, which was heated by the fire beside it. During the next quarter of a century, the efficiency of ranges improved rapidly. In 1783, in Langmead's Range, the other hob was replaced by a boiler for hot water. In 1796, an American, Count Rumford, introduced a 'stove' for heating the living rooms, which was simply a series of bricks built up around the grate to reflect the heat; and in 1802, at Rumford's instigation, Bodley's Closed Range was patented, with a cast-iron plate over the fire which acted as a hot plate and forced the rising heat into flues around the oven and the boiler.

The plumbing and sanitation, on the other hand, were as primitive as ever. When the middle classes bothered to wash themselves all over, they did it in a tub in their bedrooms. Outside the major towns, the water supply came from wells. Few, if any, of the smaller houses had water-closets. Instead, the household and its guests made do with an outside privy which was built over a cesspit in the garden. These buildings, which Isaac Ware bluntly described as 'bog houses', were usually referred to by gentlemen as 'Jericho' and were often built to look like little follies, for which, during the second half of the eighteenth century, perhaps out of respect for Palladio and the Romans, the Gothic style was regarded as particularly appropriate. John Plaw, who was fond of round buildings, produced a design for a circular Gothic privy in a pattern book published in 1795; and it was presumably privies that T. Lightoler was thinking of in 1762 when he produced a series of Gothic ruins entitled 'Façades to place before disagreeable objects'.

Most of the builders of new houses in the suburbs and countryside were, as always, gentlemen, merchants, doctors and lawyers. During the eighteenth century, however, the ranks of the fashion-conscious builders were swollen by the addition of large numbers of clergymen and a few newly rich farmers. At the beginning of the century, nearly all the clergy lived in little thatched cottages: by the end of it almost half of them were living in fine parsonages, most of which had been copied from the pattern books. In the countryside the glebe farms, from which the parsons derived a large proportion of their living, gained as much as any from enclosures and improvements in agricultural techniques. Their incomes

119. Design for a 'woodpile house' by John Plaw, 1795. Plaw's rose-embowered privy with thatch roof and Gothic doorway is in his pattern book called *Ferme Ornée or Rural Improvements*. This book includes designs for bath houses, cottages (see plate 120), Dutch barns, shepherds' huts and even a planned village.

increased, and so too did the tithes which were paid to the parsons by the other farmers in the parish. Many country parishes became capable of supporting the life-style of a modest gentleman, and as a result the Church was soon regarded as a worthy profession for a gentleman to follow. The country squires who had the right to appoint the local parson chose either a member of their own family or else the most congenial and well-bred applicant. It was an ideal job for an unambitious younger son: all he needed was an appropriate

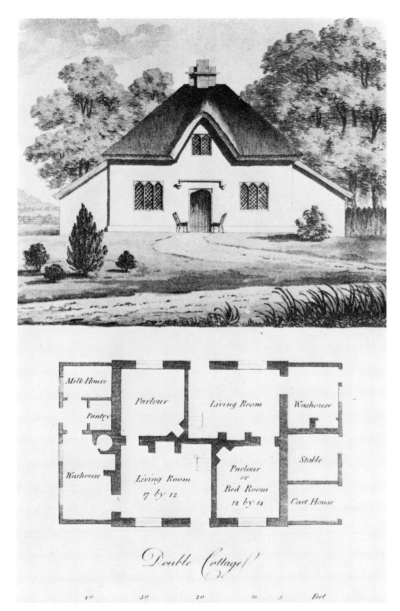

Double Cottage

120. Design for a double cottage by John Plaw, 1795. Plaw's ingenious interlocking plan for the two cottages with front doors on opposite sides of the building means that from either side it appears as one symmetrically designed cottage.

residence. Once he had built it, he could sit back and spend the rest of his life, if he chose, in comfortable and carefree idleness – and many of them chose to do exactly that.

In the more prosperous farming areas, such as East Anglia, quite a few of the surviving yeomen farmers were also much richer than their predecessors. Some were now tenants of the great estates, farming many more acres than before, but some were freeholders who had been shrewd enough to make the most out of change and progress, planting more profitable

crops and borrowing to buy land from less fortunate neighbours. Such men were no longer content to live in a timber-framed block with two rooms on each floor and share it with their labourers. Freeholders copied from the pattern books and built simple, classically proportioned farmhouses, often outside the villages as though they were little manor houses; and since the tenants were able and eager to pay larger rents for similar houses, the landlords followed the example. The rooms were usually smaller than in the earlier farm-houses, but there were now more of them, and in keeping with their new dignity they were all used by the farmer and his family. The labourers might still be fed in the kitchen during the day, but at night they were sent to sleep where they could in the barns or the lofts above the cattle sheds.

A few of the labourers on great estates were luckier – but only a few. In the second half of the eighteenth century the living conditions of the rural poor became disgraceful enough to prick even the most hardened conscience. When some of the landlords began to build new cottages, a few of the pattern books included plans for them; and in 1781, appalled by the homes of the poor around Bath, which he found to be 'shattered, dirty, inconvenient, miserable hovels, scarcely affording a shelter for the beasts of the forest,' John Wood the younger published the first pattern book devoted exclusively to cottages: *A Series of Plans for Cottages or Habitations of the Labourer.*

121. (*Above left*) Wolverton Parsonage, Hampshire, *c.* 1806.

122. Milton Abbas village, Dorset, c. 1790. This planned village resulted from Lancelot (Capability) Brown's scheme for razing the old village to the ground to make way for his landscape park around the great house in the valley below. Whether Brown or William Chambers, who designed the new house of Milton Abbey, designed these delightful cottages is as yet unknown.

In 1790, when Joseph Dormer, later Earl of Dorchester, was remodelling Milton Abbey in Dorset, he decided that the village of Milton Abbas was spoiling his view. So he knocked it down and rebuilt it elsewhere as a Classically planned village, composed of semi-detached cob and thatched cottages with Classical proportions and little rectangular doors and windows. Several other Classical model villages were built, such as the stone Lowther in Westmorland; but for many of the individual cottages the landlords applied the new tastes for Gothic or Picturesque architecture. There was no profit in this rebuilding: the tenants could not afford higher rents. Although some landlords rebuilt out of a sense of duty, some simply did it to improve the appearance of the buildings in the immediate vicinity of their mansions. A few even went so far as to construct a Picturesque hermitage and pay an eccentric simpleton to live in it.

But the new cottages were always the exception. Hovels proliferated. To be fair to the landlords, it was not in their interest to repair old cottages or build more new ones than they needed. The medieval laws, which still apply today, allowed squatters to settle in any unoccupied house they found, and since the Act of Settlement of 1662, each parish was obliged to provide relief for anyone who managed to settle in it. Since the burden of this obligation usually fell on the local landlords, many of them actually pulled down cottages to prevent anyone from using them. In the cottages that were left standing, the labourers and the married servants, who did not live in the great houses, were packed tighter than ever before. Even the pretty little cottages at Milton Abbas were each home to more than one family. In the eighteenth century the population of England almost doubled, from just over five million in 1700 to almost ten million in 1800. At the end of the century the war with Revolutionary France brought a dramatic rise in the cost of living with no commensurate rise in wages. There were thousands of homeless unemployed, and when they managed to erect a hovel without being evicted, or cover crumbling walls with thatch, they still had no way of earning a living. These were the hopeless poor who in the end migrated to the expanding towns, and if the roof they found there was any better than the wretched shelter they had left behind, the crowded life beneath it was no less miserable.

CHAPTER 8

The Town House

WHEN Inigo Jones designed the Banqueting House in 1619, London, like every other city in England, was a mass of differing half-timbered houses in narrow, dark and disordered alleys. Some jetties were so low that there was no room in the street for a cart or a carriage. The apprentices who lived in their masters' houses could lean out and shake hands across some of the most famous streets in England. With few exceptions, the only brick or stone build-

123. Carlisle in the early seventeenth century. The medieval town was dominated by its cathedral and twelfth-century castle keep, and protected, in this case against the Scots, by formidable walls. The main streets followed the lines of a much earlier layout.

ENTREE ROYALLE DE LA REYNE MERE DV ROY TRES CHRESTIEN DANS LA VILLE DE L..

124. Cheapside, London. These houses, with each floor jettied out above the floor below, were typical of town houses throughout England during the late Middle Ages.

125. Covent Garden Piazza in the early eighteenth century. Designed by Inigo Jones in 1630, it was the first square in England. On the left is his St Paul's Church, which he described as 'the finest barn in England'.

ings were palaces, churches and aristocratic mansions.

In 1630, however, with the building of Covent Garden for the Duke of Bedford, Inigo Jones introduced brick terraces. On each of his two rows of houses, the arcaded façade was one unbroken composition. There were gardens and stables in the rear, and the houses, which became London residences for the fashionable gentry, had the narrow 'dog-leg' staircases that were to remain a feature of terraced houses, and two rooms on each of four floors, with ground floors that were smaller than the others and set back to make way for the arcades. All these houses have, sadly, been replaced, but while they were being built, a neighbouring landlord, William Newton, was building Classical brick houses around Lincoln's Inn Fields, and one of these, Lindsey House, which has now been restored, is thought to have been designed by Inigo Jones.

Covent Garden was modelled on the Piazza at Livorno and the Place Royale in Paris, now the Place des Vosges. It was originally part of an ambitious plan which Inigo Jones had drawn up for redeveloping the whole area, but the Civil War

brought an end to any further building, and after the Restoration Covent Garden ceased to be a fashionable residential area. With the opening of the Drury Lane Theatre in 1663, it became the centre of London's night life instead. It was, after all, in Covent Garden that Charles II met Nell Gwynne. Some of the houses became gaming houses, and after a while the side streets were filled with taverns, coffee houses and 'bath houses'. Long before the middle of the following century, the reputation of 'the Garden' was very different. 'The first beauties of the time assembled every evening under the Piazzas,' wrote one old rake nostalgically. 'The gay scene partook of the splendour of a Venetian carnival, and such beauties as The Kitten, Peggy Yates, Sally Hall the brunette, Betsy Careless, graced the merry throng, with a hundred more, equally famed, whose names are enrolled in the cabinet of Love's votaries.'

The great impetus to the rebuilding of London was created by a catastrophe. On 3 September 1666, at the end of a long dry summer, a fire broke out in a baker's shop in Pudding Lane and spread southwards before a strong wind. For over three days it raged across four hundred acres of tight-packed timber-framed houses, from the Tower of London in the east to just short of Lincoln's Inn Fields in the west. Only the River Thames halted it to the south, and on either side it was not controlled until the citizens, under the direction of the king himself, blew up the houses in its path with gunpowder. The value of the property destroyed was estimated to be £7,000,000 – and that in a century when it had cost only £15,000 to build the magnificent Banqueting House. The fire had not purged the squalid slums where the plague that killed almost 80,000 had started in the previous year: it had swept instead through the commercial heart of the capital on either side of St Paul's Cathedral. St Paul's, despite its stone, had been damaged beyond repair; 89 churches and 13,000 houses had been burned, and nearly 200,000 people were made homeless.

On 13 September a Royal Proclamation announced that London would be rebuilt with wider streets in brick and stone. Wren, May and Pratt were appointed as commissioners, and in the following year the first Rebuilding Act was passed by Parliament: from now on, bricks and stone were required by law and houses had to have front and rear walls with a thickness equivalent to the length of two bricks. Wren drew up geometrical plans for a long quay on the banks of the Thames between the Tower of London and Blackfriars, similar to the quay on the Seine in Paris, and long wide avenues running off it and parallel to it, with churches and public buildings creating splendid vistas at their ends and junctions. But the proclamation's intention to rebuild with wide streets had not been incorporated into the Act. Freeholders refused to exchange their sites for others, and in the end the City of London was rebuilt on the same haphazard web of narrow streets that had existed before the terrible fire.

The demand for housing created a new breed of speculative builders. These men took leases on the sites from the landlords, on which they paid a nominal rent for the first year, and then they started to build houses without the money to complete them, knowing that they would find a buyer before the first year was up. At the worst, they only had to build the shell of the house before someone bought the lease off them and paid them to finish the interior to their own design and taste. Many of these speculators were craftsmen who saved money by offering their services to each other, a carpenter working on a mason's house in return for the mason working on his. Their houses were usually built in contiguous rows and were all in the Anglo-Dutch style, but the rows were not designed as one balanced composition, and even in the same row there were often houses of different sizes and heights. There are still a few of these houses standing in such streets as Bedford Row and Great Ormond Street, and one of the best examples of a row of larger houses, begun in 1678, is King's Bench Walk in the Temple, although the interiors are not typical, since they were designed as chambers for barristers.

Some of these surviving houses were built by Dr Nicholas Barbon M.P., who was by far the most successful of the new generation of speculative builders. Barbon is thought to have been the son of Praisegod Barebone, the Anabaptist, leatherseller and politician who had been a staunch supporter of Oliver Cromwell. He was an honorary Fellow of the College of Physicians and he wrote learned treatises on money, but he is best remembered for the two great fortunes that he made as a result of the Fire of London – one by being the first man in England to offer fire insurance policies, and the other by building. In general, he built long rows of identical narrow-fronted houses with kitchens in the basements, two rooms on each floor and sometimes a closet in an extension at the rear; and he was one of the first developers to fit his houses with mass-produced doors and windows.

By the standards of the time, Barbon's houses were good value and comparatively well built, but there were some ways in which he was similar to the less scrupulous developers today, or even some less scrupulous Local Authorities. Most

of his developments were outside the area that had been devastated by the fire, and he was particularly successful in the Strand, where he bought and demolished aristocratic mansions which the owners, impoverished by the Civil War and exile, were no longer able to maintain. One of these was Essex House, the London residence of the Earls of Essex, which Barbon bought from the last Earl's aunt, the Duchess of Somerset. Unfortunately, Charles II wanted to buy the house as well, and Barbon, knowing that the king could probably force him to sell it, sent his workmen to knock it down at once, and presented His Majesty with a *fait accompli*. Although he died an immensely rich man, Barbon stipulated in his will that his executors were to pay off none of his debts.

Like Barbon, several other speculators built outside the devastated area, either for the gentry or for the many merchants who no longer wanted to live in the City and risk the danger of another fire. Even before the Great Fire, London had been expanding: in 1661 the Earl of Southampton had laid out Southampton Square in front of his house in Bloomsbury and sold off some of the first building leases. But, apart from Piccadilly, where other members of the aristocracy had mansions and large gardens, the most fashionable addresses were around the Palace of Whitehall, and then the Palace of St James's after Whitehall burned down in 1698, leaving only the Banqueting House unscathed. Speculators built as close to these areas as they could, and there are still many houses beyond Whitehall, to the west of Westminster Abbey, which were built there during the last years of the seventeenth century and the first quarter of the eighteenth. The largest are double-fronted, and although they are taller than their contemporaries in the country, they are otherwise internally identical. But in the narrow, single-fronted houses, built during the eighteenth century when the English had adopted the nocturnal etiquette of the French, husbands and wives had to be content with separate apartments on separate floors.

In 1707 and 1708, while some of these houses were being built, Parliament passed additional Building Acts to limit the increasing amount of wood that was being used, particularly in the new sash windows. The wooden frames of doors and windows, which had previously been flush with the surface of the outer wall, were required to be set back at least four inches; wooden eaves, which had wooden cornices beneath them, were prohibited, and from now on the edge of the roof had to be hidden behind a brick parapet. The effect of the Acts can be seen on the surviving houses. Some of the Queen Anne houses in Queen Anne's Gate, which were built before the Acts, still

126. Houses in Queen Anne's Gate, c. 1705. The least altered street of early speculative housing, in which costs were reduced by the mass production of standardised doors, windows and interior details such as staircases.

have eaves and flush door and window frames, whereas the Georgian houses in Lord North Street, which were built around 1720, have parapets, deeper windows and much deeper doors.

Speculators even built as far out as Chelsea, where there are still a few Queen Anne houses in Cheyne Row, but the largest speculative development in London took place to the north of Piccadilly. In 1677 a Cheshire landowner, Sir Thomas Grosvenor, married the twelve-year-old Mary Davies, whose father had left her five hundred acres of farm land which then lay to the west of London. In 1720 their son, Sir Richard Grosvenor, laid out a hundred of those acres in plots around what was to become Grosvenor Square and leased them off to builders, even offering them mortgages. At the same time, other landlords were offering sites around Berkeley Square and Hanover Square. Over the next fifty years the West End of London took on the shape that it retains to this day, in a variety of Georgian houses that ranged from huge mansions in the squares through shops and terraces in the streets to tiny houses in the courts behind them, where the rooms were only twelve feet square and there was only one of them on each of the two floors.

Other towns and cities followed London's example. At the time of the Great Fire, the merchants of Bristol were developing King Street with large half-timbered houses: at the end of the seventeenth century they were building brick houses in Queen Square. With her victory in the European war, which ended in 1713, England became mistress of the seas, and within a few years she was the leading trading nation in the world. All over the kingdom the commercial centres were expanding, and new houses were being built to accommodate their growing and prosperous middle classes, who no longer wanted to live above their shops and offices. As in London, however, the first rows of new houses were only terraces in the sense that in some of them all the houses were identical. It was not until 1729, almost a hundred years after Inigo Jones designed his piazza in Covent Garden, that a new terrace was designed as one complete architectural composition, and it was built, not in London or one of the other commercial centres, but in a city whose business was pleasure – Bath.

In the seventeenth century the most fashionable spa in England had been Tunbridge Wells in Kent. By the end of the century, however, a few members of fashionable society had started to visit Bath instead, and in 1702 Queen Anne gave it the seal of royal approval by taking the waters there herself. Two years later, Beau Nash arrived from Yorkshire. At the

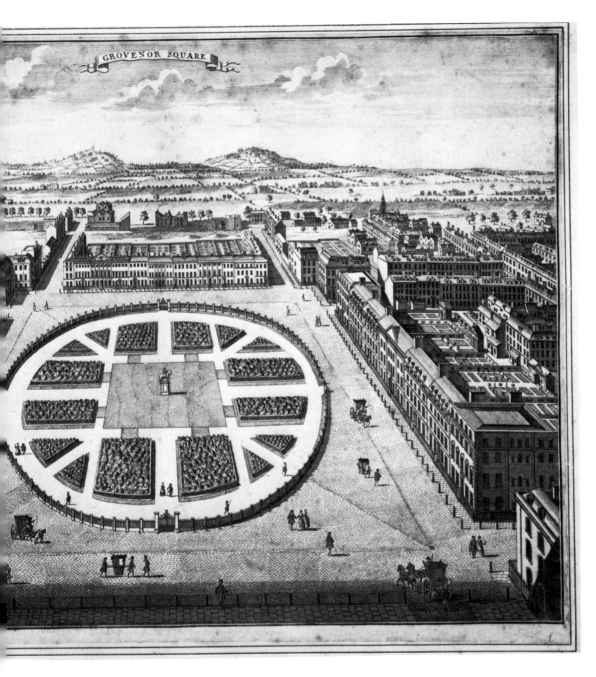

GROVENOR SQUARE.

127. Grosvenor Square, 1725–35. Unlike the Piazza at Covent Garden, the London squares of the late seventeenth century and early eighteenth century were not designed by a single architect. The houses were built either by individuals or else by speculators in small uniform groups. In Grosvenor Square, one speculator acquired the seven plots that made up the east side, but it was on the north side that another speculator, Edward Sheperd, was thwarted in his attempt to turn all his houses into a replica of a large Palladian mansion.

128. Bath. After his death in 1754, John Wood the elder's Circus was completed by his son, who later linked it to the Royal Crescent in one of the finest of all examples of town planning. Once the Woods had shown the way, others followed; and, as the most fashionable spa, Bath was particularly fortunate in the number of outstanding architects who designed its many terraces, crescents and streets later in the century.

129. Queen's Square, Bath, 1729. In Bath, John Wood the elder succeeded where Edward Sheperd had failed with Grosvenor Square in London.

time, Bath was still the medieval city that had grown up as a result of the wool trade. The only places for visitors to stay in were a few filthy boarding houses. For want of anywhere else to hold them, balls took place in the Town Hall, and the boorish 'gentlemen' who attended them came wearing their boots and swords and smoked in the presence of the ladies. But once Nash had been appointed as Master of Ceremonies, the manners and the social programme changed; and after the arrival of John Wood the elder, in 1727, Bath itself was to be transformed.

Wood had previously been working in London, where he had taken part in an unsuccessful attempt to build one side of a square as a single composition. In Bath he not only succeeded with a square, he introduced the first circus as well; and after his death his son built the first crescent. John Wood the elder drew up plans for a new 'Roman city' on the hillside overlooking the old Roman baths. It was to have a residential 'Forum' and 'Coliseum' connected by broad and splendid parades; and when it was completed it was to be the first example of large-scale town planning in England.

With financial support from Ralph Allen, Wood the elder took ninety-nine-year leases on an area to the north of the town and then sub-let plots to builders who were required to follow his designs exactly and face their houses in the stone from Allen's quarries. His first large development, begun in 1729, was the north side of Queen Square. It has a façade like a Palladian palace, with a huge pediment and engaged columns over the double-fronted house in the centre. In the elegant interiors of the houses, the less important rooms are surprisingly small and the bedchambers at the rear are very badly lit, but the tenants, who often rented them for as little as a few weeks, only used them to dine in and sleep in. Their days were spent in the theatre, the Assembly Rooms, the Pump Room, or, for form's sake, the bath, where ladies and gentlemen entered the water together in long modest bathing dresses, the ladies with little floating trays that carried their powder-puffs, scent-bottles and handkerchiefs.

The immediate success of the first terrace brought the profits to finish the square, and with continuing success the whole scheme was completed. From Queen Square, the 'Forum', at the bottom of the hill, the regularly stepped houses of Gay Street rise to the splendid Circus, the 'Coliseum', which has only two other exits, one leading to the Assembly Rooms, and the other, Brock Street, leading on through other streets to open ground, where the long Royal Crescent, situated like a gigantic country house, lies across the crest of the hill looking out over the town and the valley. Wood died just after he started to build the Circus, in 1754, and the work continued under his son, who completed Royal Crescent to his own design in 1775. John Wood the younger also built the many streets and terraces around the square and the Circus, but Bath was by then so fashionable that there were many other architects working there, including Robert Adam, who designed the shop-lined Pulteney Bridge in 1770. Several architects followed the example of the crescent: John Jelley designed Campden Crescent in 1788 and in the following year John Palmer designed Lansdowne Crescent. By the end of the century Bath was one of the most beautiful cities in northern Europe, and so much has survived that it still is.

Robert Adam's bridge in Bath was part of a large development that was never completed, but by then he and his brother James were designing the first terraces in London to be built as one architectural composition. In 1768 they leased land between the Strand and the Thames from the Duke of St Albans, drained it, built huge arcaded warehouses to create a level surface, and then built four terraces on top of them, one

130. Bedford Square, London, 1775. The first and finest square in the huge development of the Duke of Bedford's Bloomsbury estate was laid out one year after the London Building Act of 1774. This Act stipulated minimum structural standards and laid down rules governing the heights of buildings in relation to the widths of streets. The houses in Bedford Square were permitted to be higher than those in the surrounding streets. The square was built when the English landscape movement was firmly established and, unlike the earliest squares and those in European cities, it was given a garden in the centre instead of paving.

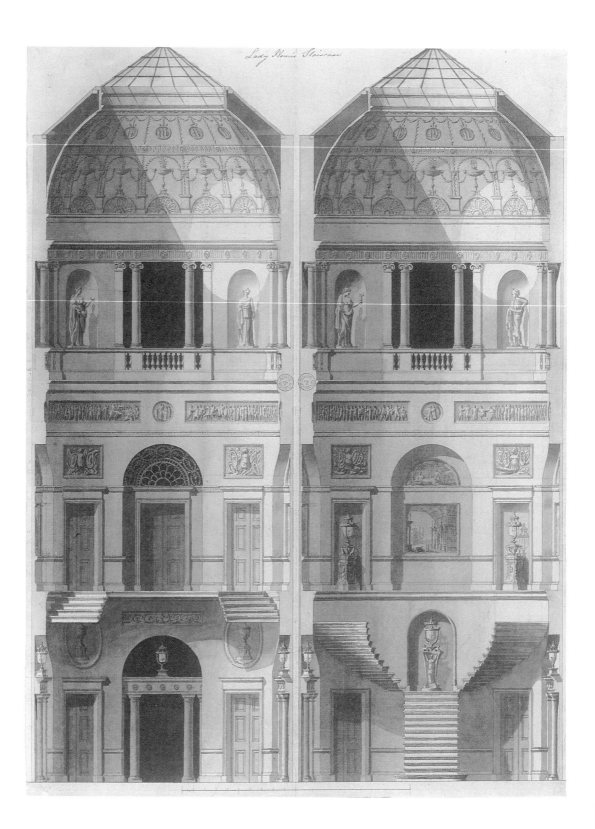

132. (*Right*) Home House, London. Design for the Etruscan Bedchamber by Robert Adam.

parallel to the river, another behind it, and two at right-angles on either side. The development, known as the Adelphi, was the most splendid in London at the time, but it was also a financial disaster for the brothers. They failed to lease the warehouses while they were building the terraces; by the time the scheme was almost complete they were over £140,000 in debt, and their creditors were not prepared to wait until all the houses were sold. In the end they only managed to save themselves from bankruptcy by holding a lottery in which the houses were prizes.

Surprisingly little of the Adam brothers' extensive building work in London has survived. Only small sections of the Adelphi are still standing, including the headquarters of the Royal Society of Arts, and there are only one or two of their houses left in Portland Place, where they were the first architects in London to use stucco. But there are two sides of Fitzroy Square which were restored externally to Robert Adam's design after being bombed in the Second World War, and one of the finest of his larger town houses, 20 Portman Square, which he designed in 1773 for the Dowager Countess of Home, is now the Courtauld Institute.

131. (*Left*) Home House, London, 1775. Robert Adam's design for the top-lit staircase. Adam designed a number of London houses, and in the larger ones, such as this, he achieved amazing effects of space within the confines of a town house.

The work of other architects of this period has fared little better, although, fortunately, one development to have survived is Bedford Square in Bloomsbury, the first square in London to be designed entirely as one composition. The land, which had originally been laid out as Southampton Square by the Earl of Southampton in 1661, came into the family of the Duke of Bedford as a dowry when the Earl's daughter Rachael married Lord William Russell, who was later executed for planning an insurrection against Charles II. Little of it had been built on, and around 1775, possibly to a design by Thomas Leverton, the fifth Duke of Bedford erected a complete square on it. The doorways are decorated in artificial Coade stone, which was manufactured to a secret and long-since forgotten formula by a Mrs Eleanor Coade of Lambeth; and the square, like most London squares, and unlike squares in Paris and other European cities, has a little, English, landscaped garden in the centre instead of paving.

Another and more obvious difference between London and Paris towards the end of the eighteenth century was that in London anyone who could afford to lived in a house, whereas in Paris even some of the aristocracy lived in apartments in huge blocks. Apart from boarding houses and the houses which became slum tenements, the only exception in London was Albany in Piccadilly, where Henry Holland extended Melbourne House, which had originally been designed by Sir William Chambers, and converted it into gentlemen's apartments.

133. Coade's Manufactory, Pedlar's Acre, London, 1798. By the time this picture was painted, the firm's catalogue listed over 778 items of artificial stone, ranging from statues and urns to ornamental plaques and capitals for columns (an Ionic capital cost 13 shillings). The firm employed a number of designers, including the architect James Paine. The patent dates from 1722, but George and Eleanor Coade's name only became associated with the firm in 1769. Despite recent analysis of the material, the secret has remained elusive since production ceased in 1837.

For the average English citizen, however, a narrow-fronted terraced house was probably much cheaper to buy or rent than an apartment would have been. Using the pattern books, the speculators were putting up houses in hundreds and selling the leases to owners or investors at very low profit-margins. In the fashionable parts of English towns today, these houses may be treasured and preserved, but there were once so many of them that the Victorians, who knocked them down in hundreds, can be forgiven for finding them monotonous. They were not very well built, either. Few speculators imagined that they

134. The Metropolitan Baths, Shepherdess Walk, Hoxton, c. 1845.

would last longer than the length of their leases. As early as 1735, Isaac Ware was complaining that some houses were so 'slightly' built that they were falling down before they were tenanted. Until the long overdue Building Act of 1774 set strict standards for even the smallest house, speculators had so little confidence in their own work that many leases included clauses prohibiting dancing on the upper floors.

For most of the eighteenth century the standards of sanitation were no better than the standards of building. There were few sewers, and the drains, which were only used for waste water, were made of brick. Although human excreta was now deposited in cesspits instead of in the street, the cesspits were usually beneath the Jerichos in the gardens or yards at the rear of the houses, and the men who came by night to empty them often had to carry their contents through the houses in buckets to their carts before dumping it in the borough cesspit or a river. It was not until after the middle of the century that terraced houses began to be fitted with internal water-closets – and at first it was a mixed blessing. It may have been more comfortable, and it may sometimes have saved the servants from emptying the commodes or chamber pots in the bedrooms, but the cesspits for these closets were often beneath the houses, seeping into the foundations and increasing the danger of typhoid by their proximity to the water supply, and since their pipes were unventilated and they had no traps, there was an added danger of being overcome by poisonous gases. It was particularly unpleasant for the servants in summer time; there was so little space in terraced houses that they not only lived in the kitchens by day, they also slept there at night in letdown beds, directly above the family cesspit.

In 1775, however, Alexander Cumming, a watchmaker of Bond Street, took out the first patent on a water-closet, which he claimed had an efficient 'stink-trap'. After that, as always, developments were rapid. In 1778 Joseph Bramah, a cabinet-maker, patented a water-closet with a similar trap but a much more effective valve for shutting off the drain. Although a cook called John Gaillait patented a complicated new stink-trap in 1782, it was Bramah's product that swept the market. Within twenty years he had sold six thousand. But he had not solved the problem – the pipes were still unventilated.

In most towns and cities the water supply came from springs or rivers. Since 1613, however, as a result of the efforts of Sir Hugh Myddleton and the New River Company, London had been supplied with water from a reservoir in Islington, which was filled from springs twenty miles away in

Hertfordshire. From this reservoir the water flowed through hollowed-out elm trunks to hand pumps in the street. During the first half of the eighteenth century, more and more houses had storage tanks in their basements that were filled by taps and lead pipes connected directly to the main wooden pipes; and during the second half, after the invention of the ball valve, these tanks were able to fill themselves as their levels fell, and shut themselves off with the valves when they were full. In those houses that boasted water-closets, the water that flushed them was pumped up by hand from the tanks into the little cisterns above them. But it was never safe to drink the water. The old wooden pipes were rotten and perforated, and the soil around them was steeped in sewage from the cesspits.

In the slums, conditions were inevitably much worse. Outside London at the end of the eighteenth century, the rural poor were flocking in thousands to find work in the new manufacturing centres. In 1700 Liverpool, Manchester, Birmingham and Sheffield were country towns with between 4,000 and 10,000 inhabitants: in 1800 they were industrial towns with between 20,000 and 100,000 inhabitants. Since wages were low, the housing for the factory workers was cheap. Landlords put up terraces of mean little two-storey houses, built back-to-back so that there was only one outside wall with a window, and that looked out over a ten-foot court to another terrace. Each court shared one pump, one privy and one cesspit. They were already so overcrowded that there was often more than one family in each room. But at least they were new. They were not yet the diseased and degrading slums that were to be the disgrace of Victorian England.

In London it was different. After the Great Fire, thousands of homeless poor had moved into the already crowded slums beyond Cripplegate, Whitechapel, Stepney and Lambeth; and since then those areas had become progressively more squalid. Cesspits were few and seldom emptied; outbreaks of cholera and typhoid were frequent; and the houses, which had once been the homes of merchants and craftsmen, were damp, dilapidated, teeming tenements.

In the fashionable West End, however, sanitary conditions changed radically at the beginning of the nineteenth century. An extensive system of sewers was built, and the old elm water pipes were taken up and replaced with pipes made of cast iron, which rusted faster than the wood had rotted. In the years between 1811 and 1830, when George IV ruled as regent and then king, the sanitary conditions in the West End of London earned it the reputation of being the cleanest city in Europe.

135. The Promenade,
Cheltenham, *c.* 1825. Between
1801 and 1826 the population of
Cheltenham increased from
3,000 to 20,000. Its rise in
popularity as a spa coincided
with Bath's decline. Cheltenham,
which remains the finest
Regency town in England, was
developed at the time when
stucco and cast-iron balconies
were the height of fashion.

These years, now known as the 'Regency', were also the last in the golden age of English Classical architecture. They were not, however, declining years. Terraces increased in both quantity and size, and although the interiors of the houses differed little from those in the previous generation, their façades were often much more elaborate. In the last quarter of the eighteenth century most brick terraces and squares had been extremely simple and restrained by the standards of the Woods' buildings in Bath. The only similarly splendid rows of houses elsewhere had been the few that were also built in stone, such as the beautiful arcaded Crescent at Buxton in Derbyshire, which was designed by John Carr in 1780. But the Regency architects created the effect of stone at a fraction of the cost by building their houses in cheap brick and facing them entirely in the new stucco. Regency terraces, crescents and squares had pediments, pilasters, colonnades, friezes and imposing porches supported by columns.

Outside London, many of the large developments were built in spas such as Cheltenham, or in the newly popular seaside resorts, where some terraces were designed with undulating rows of bow fronts and delicate wrought-iron balconies with canopies. Under royal patronage, by far the most fashionable resort was Brighton. George IV first went there when he was Prince of Wales in 1783. Three years later he commissioned Henry Holland to build him a Pavilion, and in 1815 John Nash, a former pupil of Sir Robert Taylor, began to convert it into an oriental fantasy. During the first half of the nineteenth century Brighton became as fashionable as Bath had been and expanded to include the villages of Hove and Kemp Town on either side of it. In 1825 the most prolific of the Brighton architects, Charles Busby, began to build Brunswick Terrace and Brunswick Square in Hove as one huge single composition. The long terrace on the sea front was broken in the middle by the three-sided square, which was open to the sea and had bow-fronted houses on either side.

In the same year the leading speculative builder in London, Thomas Cubitt, began to build Belgrave Square to the design of George Basevi. Cubitt was the first man to establish a modern-style building firm with all the necessary craftsmen permanently on the payroll. Before developing Belgravia on the Grosvenor estate, he had moved down through London from the north developing in parts of Highbury and St Pancras, and from Belgravia he moved on southwards to develop Pimlico and parts of Clapham. Although he sometimes modified designs to cut costs, the standard of his work was high, as is evidenced by the amount of it that has

136. Brighton, 1831. George IV and his family with the Royal Pavilion in the background. The stucco houses on the right are typical of fashionable Regency resorts, and the bay windows are particularly characteristic of the period.

FASHIONS for the SUMMER 1831 BY B. READ, Pall Mall, St James's & 12, Hart Street, Bloomsbury Sqr. LONDON.

137. The Royal Pavilion, Brighton – the Great Kitchen, 1826. The oriental fantasy of the pavilion is continued here in the design of the kitchen, where the ceiling is supported on cast-iron columns that branch out into palm leaves.

138. Carlton House, the grand staircase. Henry Holland enlarged and altered Carlton House for the Prince of Wales in 1783. Fortunately for him, he did not live to witness either Nash's transformation of his delightful neo-Classical pavilion at Brighton or the demolition in 1827 of Carlton House to make way for the steps between Nash's two blocks of Carlton House Terrace.

survived. His most impressive scheme, however, was Belgrave Square, but by the time he started to build it, work was well under way on the largest town-planning scheme to be built in London before the twentieth century. In London, the golden age was ending in a breathtaking blaze of glory.

In 1811, the year in which the Prince of Wales became regent, the leases on some farm land in Marylebone reverted to the Crown. In the following year the Prince commissioned John Nash to design a scheme that would include not only this land but also the area to the south of it. Nash did not plan the farm land as a series of squares with little landscaped gardens in their centres: he combined the Classical and Picturesque traditions to plan it as one large landscaped park, Regents

Drawn by Tho. H. Shepherd.   Engraved by W. Radcliff.

Park, surrounded by theatrical and magnificently palatial terraces. There were to be villas scattered in the park and villages of villas behind the terraces. At the southern end it was to open through a circus into the Adams' Portland Place; and to the south of Portland Place, a new street, Regent Street, was to sweep down from Oxford Circus through Piccadilly Circus to the Prince's residence, Carlton House, which was to have terraces on either side and another park, St James's Park, beyond.

When the plan was put into effect, the houses were not well built, and the decorative details were often carelessly executed by both architects and builders, but the terraces around Regents Park, and the splendid vistas that they create, are still among the most priceless treasures in London's architectural heritage. The original centrepiece, Cumberland Terrace, has three blocks joined by triumphal arches and a massive portico in the centre; the other terraces vary in style and splendour; and at the southern gate, where only half the circus was built as Park Crescent, all the porches have been joined to form one curving colonnade.

Nash never completed the scheme. Few of the villas in Regents Park were built, and much of the area which he had planned to build on around Lower Regent Street, including

139. Park Village East, London, 1824–8. John Nash originally intended to build cottages like the ones he had built twelve years earlier at Blaise Hamlet near Bristol, but the houses were finally built as miniature versions of his Italianate villas. The result was the delightful suburban backwater that still exists behind his grand terraces on the east side of Regents Park.

Drawn by Thos H. Shepherd.   Engraved by Jas Tingle.

Trafalgar Square, was still undeveloped when he died in 1835. Since then Regent Street has been completely replaced. But Nash fared far better than the two other great architects who drew up plans for London. Inigo Jones was thwarted by civil war and Sir Christopher Wren by the traditional conservatism of the City. All that remains of Jones's scheme for the land that lies to the east of Nash's are a church, some plans and a few drawings of his piazza; and all that remains of Wren's scheme for the land that lies to the east of that are a few plans and his many churches. They are enough, however, to give a picture of the London that might have been.

If only all three of them had had their way.

140. Cumberland Terrace, Regents Park, London, *c.* 1826. The most spectacular of all John Nash's great terraces overlooking the park. It was designed to look like one massive palace and was built between 1821 and 1830 under the direction of James Thomson.

CHAPTER 9

Changes in Taste

URING the first half of the eighteenth century, the English aristocracy and gentry had turned to Palladian Classical architecture under the influence of Grand Tours and books. During the second half of the century, when their taste in Classical architecture changed, it was also Grand Tours and books that changed it.

Young gentlemen and aspiring architects were not just visiting Rome and Venice to see the ruins of the ancient capital and the villas of Palladio; they were travelling throughout Italy to see other archaeological sites, such as Pompeii and the remnants of the Etruscan civilisation in Tuscany, and above all they were travelling further afield, to visit the Middle East and Greece. Encouraged in their study of archaeology by the Society of Dilettanti, which had been founded in 1733 and was led by Sir Francis Dashwood and the Earl of Middlesex, several of the young architects returned to England to publish books, to which the members of the Society subscribed. In 1753 Robert Wood published *The Ruins of Palmyra*, and four years later he published *The Ruins of Baalbec*. This was followed in 1762 by the first volume of *The Antiquities of Athens* by Nicholas Revett and James 'Athenian' Stuart, who had already designed a Greek temple for the park at Hagley. And in 1764 Robert Adam published *The Ruins of the Palace of the Emperor Diocletian at Spalato*. Together with one other architect, who did not publish under the patronage of the Dilettantis, these authors were the instigators of a new neo-Classical style, a style that sought to adhere more faithfully to the concepts of archaeological models.

The change was not as great as it might have been, however. Although the Greek civilisation was the one that was revered above all by scholars, the eighteenth-century patrons were not yet ready for the purity of Greek architecture. They might build Greek temples in their gardens, but for their houses they still preferred the more elaborate grandeur of Imperial Rome.

The other architect and author was William Chambers. Chambers's first book, published in 1757, was *Designs of Chinese Buildings, Furniture, Dresses etc*. Needless to say, this had no effect on the design of English houses, but, like the already popular Rococo style, with its graceful twisting curves and playful lack of symmetry, the Chinese taste became

141. Sir Rowland and Lady
Winn, 1770. The library at
Nostell Priory, completed in
1766–7, was the first room that
Robert Adam redecorated in
James Paine's earlier house.
Despite its unfurnished state, the
owners were impatient to display
their fashionable acceptance of
Adam's neo-Classicism and
Chippendale's magnificent desk,
which had been delivered in
1767. An almost obligatory
allusion to the grand tour, the
classical bust, has also been
placed ostentatiously in this
otherwise bare room.

fashionable for garden follies and interior decoration. Some of the best decorative examples of both are in one house, Claydon House in Buckinghamshire, which was enlarged and decorated around 1765. The ornaments around niches, doors and alcoves in the North Hall and the Chinese Room are so exquisitely delicate and brittle-looking that they appear to have been moulded out of plaster, but in fact they are wood and were carved by an otherwise unknown local carpenter called Lightfoot. Many houses were decorated with bright Chinese wallpapers, and after Chambers had built a pagoda for the dowager Princess of Wales at Kew, Chinese follies became so popular that William Halfpenny published two books on them.

But for Chambers the Chinese taste was nothing more than an amusing diversion – and a surprising one, too, for a man with little sense of humour. His second book, *A Treatise of Civil Architecture*, which was published in 1759 and included studies of the work of Bernini, Palladio and Scamozzi, was the most influential of all in spreading the taste for neo-Classicism. Chambers and his great rival, Robert Adam, whom he described as a mere interior decorator, were the leaders of the neo-Classical movement. They differed considerably in style and temperament, but, despite their less than friendly rivalry, they had more in common than neo-Classicism. They were both ambitious and, like two earlier rivals, Campbell and Gibbs, they were both Scots; and above all, like every other contemporary architect who wanted to work on country houses, they were faced with the same insurmountable problem – most of the rich aristocratic patrons already owned a Classical house. As a result, their work on large country houses was limited almost entirely to remodelling existing buildings.

Of the two, Chambers was the more eminent at the time. He was born in Sweden in 1723 and at the age of seventeen he joined the East India Company, in whose service he visited China. In 1748 he resigned and went to Paris to study architecture under the leading French neo-Classicists. On his return to England in 1755 he became architectural tutor to the Prince of Wales, later George III, and for most of his life he remained under royal patronage, rising from the office of architect to the king to become Surveyor General in 1782. He was the first Treasurer of the Royal Academy of Arts, and in 1770, after he was knighted by the king of Sweden, George III granted him the right to assume the rank and title of a knight in England. Chambers's work as a domestic architect, however, was limited to designing comparatively small houses or to the

142. Claydon House, Buckinghamshire, 1768–9. The decoration of Claydon is one of the last but also one of the most spectacular examples of English Rococo. The Rococo style had been extremely fashionable from about 1750 until the early 1760s, when Adam's neo-Classical decoration imposed a more serious attitude on English taste. It was essentially frivolous and exotic, and in the North Hall and the Chinese Room (overleaf) at Claydon it reached an extraordinary level of fantasy. Most Rococo decoration was carried out in stucco, but here, astonishingly, it was all carved in wood by a mysterious genius called Mr Lightfoot.

143. Detail from the Chinese Room, Claydon House.

frustrating compromise of remodelling and extending existing Palladian buildings. His influence was spread more through his second book and his followers than through his houses. In 1776, twenty years before his death, when he began work on the huge block of government offices that was to replace the old Somerset House and was to be the largest public building erected in London since the Royal Naval Hospital, he gave up working for private clients. Like Melbourne House, now Albany, most of his houses have been greatly altered, but there are still a few survivors, such as Pepper Harrow in Surrey.

144. The State Drawing-Room, Syon House, Middlesex, 1762–9. Robert Adam's sequence of state rooms at Syon must rank among his finest achievements. It is obvious in these magnificent rooms that one man is in control of all the decoration down to the smallest detail, from the elaborate designs for ceiling and carpet to the exquisitely fine ormolu decoration on the marble chimneypiece.

145. The Hall, Syon House. Adam was obliged to work within the old structure of the Tudor house, which presented endless problems to an architect determined to provide rooms with correct Classical proportions. In the great Entrance Hall he formed apses at either end to reduce the length of the main body of the room to the proportions of a double cube, and he used one to disguise a change of level as well.

146. The Ante Room, Syon House. Here, Adam turned the old rectangular room into a square by creating a screen at one end, opposite the door from the Hall, with four antique columns which had been found in the bed of the River Tiber. Green, gold, blue and terracotta colours predominate in this sumptious room.

Robert Adam, on the other hand, was the busiest domestic architect of his generation. Born the son of a Scots architect in 1728, he went on the Grand Tour in 1754 and returned to England four years later to set up in architectural practice with his brother James as his draughtsman and business manager. In his designs for the exteriors of country houses, Robert Adam varied the proportions of his Classical features in accordance with the needs of the existing buildings, and in total disregard for the Palladian rules, creating a lightness and a movement that were often missing in Palladian houses. But, despite the jibe of Sir William Chambers, it was with his interior decoration that he was to alter English taste entirely.

Like William Kent, he varied the shapes of his rooms, designed their furniture and supervised every detail of the work; and he replaced the solemn Palladian ornament with merry and subtle decorations that were drawn from a variety of Classical sources. In the preface to the first volume of *The Works in Architecture of Robert and James Adam Esquires*, which was published in 1773, he wrote boastfully but truthfully:

> The massive entabulature, the ponderous compartment ceiling, the tabernacle frame, almost the only species of ornament formerly known in this country, are now universally exploded, and in their place we have adopted a beautiful variety of light mouldings, gracefully formed, delicately enriched, and arranged with propriety and skill.

There are many great houses in England which were altered and decorated by Robert Adam. In 1760 he worked on the Jacobean Osterley Park in Middlesex for a banker called Robert Child, cutting through its entrance front into the courtyard with a portico and giving it one of his most famous

Etruscan rooms, in which the decorations were taken from Greek vases which were then thought to be Etruscan. In the following year he started work for Sir Hugh Smithson, later first Duke of Northumberland, on nearby Syon House, where the austere castellated façades contain a series of magnificently opulent rooms, including an enchanting long gallery, which Adam said that he had 'finished in a style to afford great variety and amusement'. And among the finest of his other houses are Harewood House in Yorkshire, Luton Hoo in Bedfordshire and Kenwood House in Middlesex, which has a beautiful and at the time unusual barrel-vaulted library.

But Adam also designed one exterior which was more significant than he may have realised. Although the house itself created no change, Adam's approach to its design was soon to be the basis of an entirely new taste in architecture. In 1760, for Sir Nathaniel Curzon, later Lord Scarsdale, he started work on the completion of the central block at Kedleston Hall in Derbyshire, which had been begun by James Paine. The flanking pavilions, then already built by Paine and Matthew Brettingham, are Palladian, but Adam's garden front of the central block is reminiscent of Vanbrugh, and its 'movement', which was intended to create the same effect as 'swelling and sinking have in landscape', was described by Adam as 'Picturesqueness'.

Among the many architects who designed interiors in Robert Adam's style, the most fashionable was James Wyatt. In 1780 Wyatt was commissioned by Sir Gerard Vanneck, later Lord Huntingfield, to design the interior of Heveningham Hall in Suffolk, which was being rebuilt to a design by Sir Robert Taylor. Some of Wyatt's earlier interiors had been so close to Adam's that Adam had accused him of plagiarism, and at Heveningham they are still very similar. Wyatt even gave the hall a barrel-vaulted ceiling. But there is one important difference in that hall, and it is not a difference that was limited to Wyatt's work alone. There is one decorative element that does not derive from Classical sources. The imitation fan vaulting comes from a style which was rising in fashion concurrently with neo-Classicism – Gothic.

The Gothic style had never entirely died out in England. At Oxford, for example, during the late seventeenth century, Sir Christopher Wren had designed the Gothic Tom Tower for Christ Church, and during the early eighteenth century Nicholas Hawksmoor had designed Gothic buildings for All Souls. But the Gothic style was not appropriate for houses at times when social custom required internal symmetry or when the Rule of Taste reigned supreme. With the growing

147. The Long Gallery, Syon House. Adam's treatment of the uncompromising proportions of the Tudor gallery, which is 136 feet long but only 14 feet wide, is shown in this engraving of his design.

148. The Roman Closet, Syon House. At either end of the gallery, Adam created two closets in the old turrets of the Tudor house. The Roman closet reveals his genius for designing a neo-Classical interior on a miniature scale – this supremely elegant circular room is less than 10 feet in diameter.

interest in archaeology, however, educated gentlemen were also studying the ancient buildings of their own culture, and at the same time, with the rejection of the French plan, the internal shapes of their houses were changing. There was no longer any reason other than tradition for having the principal rooms on the first floor. After the middle of the eighteenth century many Classical houses, such as Chambers's Pepper Harrow, were being built with their principal rooms on the ground floor; and by the end of the century this was almost universal. In these houses the servants' hall and kitchens were either in the basement or else, where there was no basement, in one of the wings. But the other wing served no practical or social purpose: in a Classical house it was simply there for the sake of external symmetry. The only thing that now prevented a romantically inclined gentleman from building an asymmetrical Gothic house was a fear of being out of fashion. Once one of the leaders of fashion had done it, a few, tentatively, followed his example.

The Gothic taste was used on the interiors of a number of houses during the 1740s, including St Michael's Mount in Cornwall and Malmesbury House in Wiltshire, and it was also used for a number of follies, but the house that was probably

149. The south front of Kedleston Hall, Derbyshire, 1758–68. The central feature of this façade, designed by Robert Adam, is based on the design of a Roman triumphal arch, a theme that appears in a number of neo-Classical houses. (Adam was in Rome during the 1750s when new excavations were revealing a number of Classical buildings, which he would have been able to study at eye-level as they emerged.)

150. Heveningham Hall, Suffolk, 1778–84. James Wyatt's finest interior shows him as the natural heir to Robert Adam. Here he has used a barrel-vaulted ceiling, developing it into a miraculously intricate design and introducing imitation Gothic fan vaulting amidst the otherwise Classical decorations.

151. Strawberry Hill, 1747–76. Unlike James Wyatt, who designed a great number of Gothic houses in a serious vein, Adam produced Gothic decorations in the frivolous tradition of the Rococo. His work is exemplified here in the cornice and ceiling which he designed for Horace Walpole's round tower in the most famous of all the eighteenth-century Gothic Revival houses.

the first to be built in the Gothic style, and certainly the most famous, was Strawberry Hill in Middlesex. In 1747, Horace Walpole, a leader of fashion, bought an existing house from a Mrs Chevenix and turned it into a little Gothic castle. He did not, however, design it as a serious reproduction of a medieval Gothic house. It was intended to be an amusing folly. Several leading architects advised him, including Robert Adam, who designed the round tower; and with their help he created a fantasy, with crenellations, tall chimneys and oriel windows on the outside, and screens, chimneypieces shaped like tombs, and delicate plaster fan vaulting in rooms with practical Georgian proportions.

The fashion for Gothic architecture took off slowly. In 1750, while Walpole was building Strawberry Hill, Sir Roger Newdigate began to remodel his Tudor house, Arbury Hall in Warwickshire, with the help of Sanderson Miller and others.

152. Arbury Hall, Warwickshire, 1750–1800. As at Horace Walpole's more famous Strawberry Hill, the Gothicising of Arbury began as Rococo embellishment. Over the years, however, a more serious archaeological attitude towards the medieval style was adopted. The beautiful plasterwork of the fan vaulting in the saloon was carried out by W. Hanwell in 1786.

The interior is extravagantly Gothic, but the exterior, for all its Gothic decoration, is still totally symmetrical. For a while this was as far as the fashion went. Although Gothic features were used increasingly on the exterior of houses, the builders clung faithfully to Classical proportions. Many smaller houses were altered and given Gothic shapes to their square-paned sash windows. Some were embellished with stucco oriels, and there were even a few which were given Gothic arches over the centre of Venetian windows. At Beccles, in Suffolk, a new house, St Peter's House, was built with a Classical pedimented front and a Gothic façade overlooking the garden; and at the other end of the scale a number of the old half-timbered houses which had not been 'modernised' with plaster or stucco and rectangular windows were now given 'a more authentic medieval look' with arched Gothic windows instead.

There were quite a few new, asymmetrical Gothic villas, such as Donnington Grove in Berkshire, which was designed around 1760, probably by John Chute, and was later enlarged by its new owner, William Brummel, the father of the great Regency dandy Beau Brummel. But it was not until 1772 that a Shropshire squire, Richard Payne Knight, turned his house, Downton Castle, into the first large, asymmetrical Gothic mansion. After that the taste for larger Gothic houses spread, and in 1796 James Wyatt designed the largest of them all for William Beckford, an immensely rich and eccentric West Indies merchant who once wrote a novel in French, *Vathek*, in three consecutive days and nights. Beckford's house, Fonthill Abbey in Wiltshire, was a massive, rambling pile, set high up on the downs and crowned by a gigantic 225-foot tower – which collapsed twice.

153. A caricature of 1807 showing a small library with Gothic glazing and a Gothic desk.

A BRACE of FULL-GROWN PUPPIES : or MY DOG and ME.

154. East Cowes Castle, Isle of Wight, *c.* 1798. By the time he began to build East Cowes Castle for himself, John Nash had been influenced by the Picturesque movement and was a friend of its leading advocate, Richard Payne Knight, who had built his own castle, Downton in Herefordshire, between 1772 and 1778. Nash may also have decided to build the house as a castle because his rival, James Wyatt, was building Norris Castle on the Isle of Wight at the same time.

Richard Payne Knight was the author of *An Analytical Inquiry into the Principles of Taste*, in which he argued that the word 'Picturesque', which had previously been applied only to landscaped gardens, came from the Italian *pittoresco*, 'after the manner of painters', and could be applied equally to architecture. Like a castle in a romantic painting, Downton was designed as part of the landscape in which it was set, and its lack of symmetry and mixture of styles were intended to reflect that landscape. In its own grandiose way, Fonthill followed the example, and during the Regency many more Gothic and Picturesque castles were built, particularly by John Nash, who designed among others Knepp in Sussex, Luscombe in Devon and his own castle at East Cowes on the Isle of Wight.

155. Fonthill Abbey, Wiltshire, 1796. James Wyatt's enormous folly was built for William Beckford, whose wealth fortunately matched his eccentricity. This enormous Gothic house was designed to rival Salisbury Cathedral, although the huge spire that Wyatt designed for it was never built. The 225-foot tower collapsed in 1800 before the house was finished and was immediately rebuilt. Another collapse was averted when it was rebuilt again in stone in 1806, but even then it only lasted for nineteen years. When it collapsed for the last time in 1825, it demolished part of the house as well.

The Regency vogue for Picturesque architecture was not confined to Gothic castles. At the height of its fashion the style produced some of the weirdest houses in England. Around 1820 The Jungle in Lincolnshire was built for Samuel Russell Collett, who kept a menagerie. One front of this otherwise Classical house is designed to look like a ruined castle from a fairy tale. Most of the windows are Gothic and framed in twisted branches of oak, but some of them, together with one of the doors, are shaped to look like knots in a tree-trunk.

With the exception of follies, however, the majority of the Picturesque buildings were cottages. Many were labourers' cottages, like the romantic *cottages ornés* at Blaise Hamlet, now in Avon, which were again designed by John Nash. But there was also a fashion among the gentry for building larger and inconveniently Picturesque cottages as country retreats. It was this fashion that Jane Austen was mocking in the speech that she wrote for the foolish Robert Ferrars in *Sense and Sensibility*: 'I am excessively fond of a cottage; there is always so much comfort, so much elegance about them.'

156. Blaise Hamlet, *c.* 1822.
Nash designed this group of nine
cottages in 1811. Like castles,
cottages such as these were
among the most fashionable
expressions of the Picturesque
movement.

157. An 1816 watercolour of the
'cottage' on the Isle of Wight
which was for ten years the
home of Thomas Bowdler, the
expurgator of Shakespeare, who
gave the word 'bowdlerize' to
the English language. There was
a considerable vogue at the
beginning of the nineteenth
century for designing quite large
houses in the style of cottages.
The most famous was the Prince
Regent's cottage in Windsor
Park, which was designed by
Nash in 1813 and subsequently
rebuilt in early-Victorian times
and renamed Royal Lodge.

John Nash, the designer of cottages and castles, was the most fashionable and prolific Regency architect. He went bankrupt when he first set up in practice, after leaving Sir Robert Taylor's office, but after a more successful period in Wales, he returned to London in 1796, at the age of 44, and went into partnership with the landscape architect Humphrey Repton. Two years later, he married a young lady who was a very close friend of the Prince of Wales, and four years after that, under the prince's patronage, he set up in practice on his own again. Nash could design in a variety of styles, from the neo-Classicism of some of his terraces to Gothic castles or the Oriental style of the Royal Pavilion. His work was never admired by scholars, and he himself admitted that his details were bad. 'Never mind,' he once said of an ill-adjusted sketch, 'it won't be observed in the execution.' But at Southborough Place in Surrey he created the epitome of the Regency house, and his enchanting Picturesque Italian villas with round towers, arched loggias and conical roofs, such as Cronkill in Shropshire and Sandridge Park in Devon, were the forerunners of many others, none of which managed to match his delicacy.

158. Cronkhill, Shropshire, c. 1802. This is the most Italianate of all Nash's houses. Like all Picturesque houses, it has an asymmetrical plan. The round tower is no more than a dramatic piece of composition: the only room inside it that is circular is the one at the top. Nash's Italianate houses and villas were the precursors of countless others in the early-Victorian suburbs.

'Fashionable society', for which Nash designed, had changed greatly since the days before the Napoleonic Wars. Membership now depended more on wit and charm than on rank and fortune. Behind the balls and the assemblies, the social life was courteously informal, and the social programme of the day was longer. Hostesses received guests for tea or coffee during the day in morning-rooms and drawing-rooms and gave smaller but more frequent dinner parties in the evenings. The dinners were now served at 6.30 or 7.00 p.m., and all the gentlemen who attended them, following the example of Beau Brummel, wore black tailcoats and white stocks. Country houses were now much closer in layout to the houses of the twentieth century: they were designed to a variety of plans, and now that the principal rooms were on the ground floor, the family bedrooms were on the floor above instead of beside them. Despite the castles, most country houses were smaller than they had been in the previous century. Aristocratic fortunes were few, and the Napoleonic Wars had created a shortage of building materials. But although their houses were often cheaply built and stuccoed, the Regency clients still required them to appear as elegant and imposing as possible. In Regency England style was everything. The world of Beau Brummel was a world of immaculate façades, and for such a world John Nash was the ideal architect.

159. Grange Park, near Alresford, Hampshire, c. 1810. A seventeenth-century house was here remodelled in the severest manner of the Greek Revival by William Wilkins for the banker Henry Drummond. The house, shown here before its most recent restoration, was extended in 1823 by S. P. Cockerell and again in 1852 by his son, C. R. Cockerell. The portico was derived from the Thesion in Athens.

160. 12 Lincoln's Inn Fields, London, 1792. The breakfast-room in Soane's own house (now Sir John Soane's Museum) displays the same refined elegance that he brought to the design of his houses.

The most imaginative and original Regency architect was Sir John Soane. Soane's houses, such as Aynhoe in Northamptonshire, Moggerhanger in Bedfordshire, or his own house in Lincoln's Inn Fields, which he converted into an architectural museum, were all designed in a Greek-influenced fusion of the neo-Classical and the Picturesque. He still used Roman models, however. At Pitzhanger Manor, now Ealing Public Library, which he bought as a country house in 1800, he rebuilt George Dance's original house and based the front on the Roman Arch of Constantine, which had been Robert

INTERIORS

161. Illustrations from Humphrey Repton's *Fragments*, 1816. From 1797 to 1802 the partnership of Repton, the landscape gardener, and Nash, the architect, produced some of the most successful examples of the whole Picturesque style. Here, in this book, Repton is contrasting the dull formality of a Classical room with the informal grouping of people in a light and airy room leading into a conservatory.

Adam's model for Kedleston.

The neo-Classical tradition had reached its logical conclusion. Greek friezes and columns were now being used on the façades and porches of stuccoed terraces. Some patrons were even building entirely Greek country houses. The purest was Belsay Castle in Northumberland, which was begun in 1807 by Sir Charles Monk, who had spent his honeymoon studying the temples in Greece; and the largest was Grange Park in Hampshire, designed by William Wilkins in 1810. But the Greek influence produced the most successful designs when

combined with the Palladian tradition: now that the principal rooms were on the ground floor, the columns for their porticos could rise, as they did in Greece, from the base. Such a house is Dinton House in Wiltshire, which was designed in 1813 by Jeffrey Wyatt, the nephew of James Wyatt, who changed his name to Wyatville after being knighted for rebuilding Windsor Castle. Dinton is one of the last of the Classical English country houses, and in its sheer confident simplicity it is also one of the loveliest.

The Regency architects designed in many styles, and in their Picturesque houses in particular they borrowed from many other traditions, such as Egyptian, Arabic and Indian. They often built carelessly and mixed their styles unsuccessfully, but they built with a delicacy and wit that would not have offended Adam or Walpole. At their best, they were not unworthy successors to the great architects of the golden age, and they left the Victorians a rich variety of well-trodden roads to follow. But the Victorians did not tread lightly.

162. 'The Warm Bath', an Ackermann print of 1812, showing a remarkably modern-looking bath with hot and cold taps.

163. Corinthian villa from *Retreats, A Series of Designs, consisting of plans and elevations for cottages,* 1827. By the time this beautifully illustrated pattern book was published, the less-gifted architects, of whom the author was obviously one, were in a quandary as to what style to present to the public. The seeds of confusion are already evident in this design.

CORINTHIAN VILLA.

164. House in Chapel Street, Penzance, Cornwall. The Egyptian style became extremely fashionable for furniture after Napoleon's campaign in Egypt and Nelson's victory at the Nile in 1798. For houses, however, it was the most bizarre and least adopted of the Picturesque styles. This house includes the Napoleonic eagle as well as the Royal coat of arms among its decorations.

165. The Conservatory, Carlton
House, 1807. This large Gothic
conservatory was added to
Carlton House for the Prince
Regent by Thomas Hopper.

CHAPTER 10

Victorian Confusion

T HE reign of Queen Victoria, like the reign of Queen Elizabeth I, was an age of vast 'prodigy houses'. After a slow start, it was a period of rapid and uninterrupted industrial growth. The agricultural slump that had followed the Napoleonic Wars had in turn been followed by a boom. The aristocracy were again earning fortunes from farming, and many of them were earning more than ever from the suburbs that were built on their land or the minerals that lay beneath it. By the time the agricultural economy declined, during the last quarter of the nineteenth century, the profits had been invested in industry. Once more the great land-owners were building new houses, and so too, in equal numbers, were the owners of ships, foundries, mills and factories.

The political influence which accompanied the ownership of land had diminished after the Reform Bill of 1832, which gave the vote to leaseholders and other country tenants paying more than £50 a year. But the ownership of a house in the country was still the only road to social recognition, if not for the first generation of *nouveaux riches,* then at least for the leisured sons and grandsons that they sent to be educated at Eton and Harrow. Like the 'new men' of the Elizabethan age, they built their houses as symbols of their wealth and earned their peerages and influence by engaging in the political arena themselves. The Tory Prime Minister Sir Robert Peel, who was educated at Harrow and Christ Church, Oxford, was the son of a Lancashire cotton manufacturer and lived at Drayton Manor in Staffordshire. The Liberal Prime Minister William Ewart Gladstone, who was educated at Eton and Christ Church, was the son of a Liverpool slave trader and lived at Hawarden Castle in Flintshire. And both had sons who served in governments and were elevated to the peerage.

The Industrial Revolution which had brought the wealth to build on the scale of the Elizabethans also brought the means to build more easily. Towards the end of the eighteenth century, canals had been used for transporting those bricks that were not actually baked on site; but during the first half of the nineteenth century the greatly expanded canal system was carrying not only bricks but stone, slate, tiles and imported marble, and during the second half of the century the railways

were carrying them faster and more cheaply. The stone that had once been cut into blocks by hand was now cut by steam-powered machines. The local masons who carved it and the other self-employed craftsmen who had traditionally built country houses were gradually replaced by teams of employees from large firms. By 1880 nearly all the large houses were being built by William Cubitt and Son or one of the construction firms that had been set up after it, such as Trollope and Sons.

The rich Victorian clients rejected the sham stucco of the Regency and faced their houses in stone and many differing colours of brick, but they used more modern materials as well. Concrete, developed in the 1830s, was sometimes used for foundations and floors, and at one house, Down Hall in Essex, which was designed by E. P. Cockerell in 1871, the whole structure was made of concrete poured into moulds and

166. Bear Wood, Berkshire, 1865. Robert Kerr's heavy-handed imitation of Elizabethan architecture.

reinforced with strips of iron. Iron had been used to support the staircases in a few Regency houses, such as the Royal Pavilion, but in many Victorian houses there was a great deal more of it. Broad roofs and ceilings, which had previously been spanned in timber and stone by ingenious carpenters and masons, were spanned instead with iron beams by engineers. Conservatories, which became almost as obligatory as libraries, were created out of wrought iron and large sheets of plate glass. At first the new plate glass was extremely expensive, since it was subject to a tax which was measured by weight. After the tax was abolished in 1845, however, window-panes became increasingly larger; and after the abolition of window tax in 1851, the windows in smaller houses became more numerous.

The trains which carried these materials also carried the members of the large and frequent house parties which helped to justify the size of the houses. In order to accommodate these guests, together with their ladies' maids and valets, the Victorian country house required not only many bedrooms but many rooms that could be used during the day as well. In 1864 the architect Robert Kerr outlined the design and organisation appropriate to such an establishment in *The Gentleman's House; or How to Plan English Residences, from the Parsonage to the Palace*; and in the following year he designed Bear Wood in Berkshire for John Walter, the leading proprietor of *The Times*.

Bear Wood exemplified his ideas, and in many ways, including taste, it was typical of Victorian country houses. On the ground floor the long list of rooms included a drawing-room, a morning-room, a library, a picture gallery, a gentlemen's library which could be used as a smoking-room, a dining-room, a billiard-room, a gun-room, a deed-room and a waiting-room for those who came to see the master on business. And yet, by the standards of many, Bear Wood was a modest house: its hall was hardly a great hall, and it had no ballroom, no chapel, no study, no breakfast-room.

Kerr divided the rooms into masculine and feminine: the drawing-room, for example, was feminine, the billiard-room, and also the dining-room, were masculine. Apart from the principal staircase in a tower, there was a gentlemen's staircase in a turret beside it. On the first floor, the master and his wife had separate apartments, into which they would retire from their guests and from each other, and in keeping with the moral tone of the times, the bachelors' bedrooms and those for young ladies were set at opposite ends of the house.

'The family constitute one community,' wrote Kerr, 'the

167. Passage leading to the Gothic library, Stowe, 1807. Sir John Soane designed the library in 1805. This painting shows the endless stone-flagged passages that were required to service the principal rooms in large houses.

168. Three mid-nineteenth-century rooms:
(*Left*) A town house bedroom.
(*Below, left*) A kitchen in a country house.
(*Below*) A London drawing-room.

servants another.' There could be as many as fifty indoor servants in a great Victorian country house, but they lived in their own hierarchical and rigidly disciplined worlds. The family and their guests were unaware of most of them: the only servants that they saw were the butler, the housekeeper, the footmen, the parlourmaids, the nursemaids who looked after their children, and their own personal ladies' maids and valets. The chefs, pastry cooks, kitchen maids, laundry maids, bootboys and many others never ventured beyond the doors of the servants' wing; and those who cleaned and tidied and polished, such as housemaids and chamber maids, only crossed the social boundary when the family and their guests were in bed or at table.

A Victorian servants' wing was as large as many a Georgian mansion. At Bear Wood it was almost a third of the house. Separate male and female staircases led to well-segregated sleeping quarters, and beneath these the rooms were divided

into different domains under the command of the butler, the chef and the housekeeper. The mens' corridor lay beyond the dining-room and the butler's pantry, with the plate safe and the butler's bedroom on one side and the footmen's room and various cleaning rooms on the other. At right-angles to this corridor, the housekeeper's corridor ran out past the servants' hall along one side of the kitchen court, with the housekeeper's room at the end beyond a store-room, a still-room and a women's work-room; and beyond the servants' hall, the larder, pantries, kitchen and scullery extended round the rest of the kitchen court to sheds, coal-houses, a boiler-room and the engine-room that contained the steam pump for the water.

Since Bear Wood was a comparatively modest house, the social segregation among the servants was limited by the number of rooms available to them. Butler, chef, housekeeper and personal servants ate breakfast and tea in the house-keeper's room and dined and supped in the servants' hall with the others. But in the largest houses, where there was often a steward instead of a butler, the senior servants ate in the steward's room and sometimes had separate sitting-rooms of their own. A career 'in service' was not unattractive during the nineteenth century. The pay was low and the hours were long, but they were not much better elsewhere, and the living conditions, however limited, were far more comfortable and clean than the squalid cottages and back-to-back slums of many farm labourers and factory workers.

Bear Wood was set in a park and screened by acres of equally unattractive evergreen conifers. The Victorian obsession with privacy went far beyond a desire to be undisturbed by lower servants. Unlike the rich Georgians, whose houses could be seen from the road and were open to the genteel public, the rich Victorians hid most of their houses beyond trees and did not feel inclined to share their taste, or lack of it, with strangers. During the reign of Queen Victoria there were very few country houses where the housekeepers were burdened with the added duty of showing them to passing ladies and gentlemen.

But there were other more important ways in which the Victorians differed from the Georgians. The Victorians took life and themselves more seriously. Theirs was an age of paradox and double standards. Although it was an age of religious revival, it was also, towards the end, an age of growing Darwinian agnosticism. The aristocracy and *nouveaux riches* ensured that their servants prayed every morning, and they set great store by their families, their homes and the Puritan ethos. But secretly their sexual morals were no

169. Scarisbrick Hall, Lancashire, 1837. Designed by Augustus Welby Pugin at the age of 24, Scarisbrick was a brave attempt to recreate a medieval manor house on the foundations of an earlier house. The original composition was later dwarfed by the insensitive addition of the tower by Pugin's son Edward.

better than any other generation's, and their single-minded pursuit of wealth was in general accompanied by a shameful indifference to the suffering of those who produced it.

To such men, Classical domestic architecture was the architecture of the decadent Regency; the style might be suitable in its purest form for public or commercial buildings, but it was morally inappropriate for houses. They did not, on the other hand, regard Gothic architecture as similarly tainted. With its affinities to ecclesiastical architecture and its aura of the age of chivalry, the Gothic style appealed to both pious aristocrats and socially ambitious industrialists who sought to surround themselves with the trappings of an ancient heritage. But Victorian Gothic was not the delicate and often picturesque pastiche of the Regency: it was a serious attempt to recreate medieval architecture on a larger scale. Victorian Gothic houses were more solid-looking, and as time passed they became heavier and heavier.

The architect who established the Gothic taste in Victorian England was Augustus Welby Northmore Pugin. He was the son of a French refugee who had worked as a draughtsman in John Nash's office and had published a Gothic pattern book, *Specimens of Gothic Architecture*, in 1821. Following in his father's footsteps, Pugin believed passionately that the Middle Ages were the peak of Christian civilisation and that Gothic was the only true architecture of Christianity. In 1834, at the age of twenty-two, he converted to Roman Catholicism, and although he designed a few uncompromisingly Gothic houses, most of his buildings were Catholic churches. During his short but productive life, he worked so obsessively that by the time he died, at the age of forty, he was mad.

In 1836 Sir Charles Barry won the competition to become the architect of the new Houses of Parliament with a plan in which the Gothic decorations had been designed by the young Pugin. In the same year Pugin published *Contrasts: or a Parallel between the noble edifices of the fourteenth and fifteenth centuries and similar buildings of the present day. Showing the present decay of Taste.* In this pamphlet Pugin attempted to prove the decadence and inferiority of Renaissance buildings by comparing them with medieval examples; and a few years later, in *True Principles of Pointed or Christian Architecture*, he condemned the sham Gothic of Wyatt and abhorred the fashion for Picturesque architecture. A house, he argued, should look like a house and not a castle: its external appearance should be dictated by its function. But Pugin was a man of his times; he did not entirely follow his own principles in practice. His attempts to recreate medieval manor houses were undoubt-

170. Knightshayes Court, Devon, 1869. A design by William Burges for the interior. At the same time he was working on the spectacular interiors for Cardiff Castle.

171. (*Right*) Eaton Hall, Cheshire, 1804 and 1870. The comparison between these two interiors in the same house could scarcely be more telling. The lightness of the Gothic house designed by William Porden in 1804 was transformed into the gloom of mid-Victorian Gothic by Alfred Waterhouse when he carried out extensive alterations and additions in 1870 at a cost of £600,000.

edly Picturesque; they contained great halls with no other justification than the fact that they were authentic and could be used by their owners for entertaining tenants and servants at Christmas; and one of them was even a castle.

In 1837, Charles Scarisbrick, a rich Catholic recluse, commissioned Pugin to remodel Scarisbrick Hall in Lancashire. The interior is overwhelmingly ornate and the exterior is much less convincingly medieval than it was in the original sketch which Pugin prepared before building began. Even the sketch contained a little clock tower, however, and in 1860, after both Pugin and his client were dead, Scarisbrick's sister engaged Pugin's son, E. W. Pugin, to replace it with the disproportionately tall and slender tower which now dominates the whole building. The house has little of the practicality and lack of pretension which Pugin had advocated so vehemently, but it was not nearly as Picturesque as his next great house, Alton Castle, in Staffordshire, which he designed in 1847 for the Earl of Shrewsbury and set dramatically on a cliff top.

Between 1850 and 1870, Gothic was the most popular style among the gentry and aristocracy. Most of them commissioned architects who specialised in country houses, but a few of their houses were designed by the most eminent Gothic architects, such as Sir George Gilbert Scott and Alfred Waterhouse, whose practices were more concerned with churches and public buildings. In 1858 Scott designed the scholarly and unimpressive Kelham Hall in Nottinghamshire for John Henry Manners-Sutton; and in 1870 Waterhouse rebuilt Eaton Hall with another clock tower for Hugh Lupus Grosvenor, first Duke of Westminster and owner of the rich estates in London which had been developing steadily since the early eighteenth century. By the time Kelham was designed, Gothic houses were already putting on weight, but although Kelham and Eaton were solid and unattractive, they were not as cumbersome as many. William Burges's Knightshayes Court in Devon and S. S. Teulon's Elvetham Hall in Hampshire, for example, were positively corpulent.

With the support of the great art critic John Ruskin, who proclaimed its moral superiority, Pugin had succeeded in his effort to spread the gospel of Gothic architecture. But he was not so successful in his less convincing attempt to suppress the taste for Picturesque castles. William Burges designed two in Wales, and Anthony Salvin, a former pupil of John Nash, designed several in England, including Scotney Castle in Kent and parts of a real castle, Alnwick in Northumberland. Salvin's most splendidly Picturesque castle, however, was

1493. Eaton Hall. Ante-Drawing Room.

Peckfirton Castle in Cheshire, which he designed in 1844 for Lionel Tollemache, later Lord Tollemache, a fervent Christian and one of the few moralising Victorians who practised what he preached. He built over fifty new farmhouses for his tenant farmers and provided each of his 250 farm labourers with a new cottage and three acres of land.

Salvin also designed for clients who wanted to build in the style of the more recent past. Appropriately, a few of the *nouveaux riches* and a growing number of the less outwardly pious aristocracy and gentry preferred to model their houses on the great houses of the Elizabethans. The first 'Tudor' houses had been built during the Regency: in 1808 James Wyatt had designed the spectacularly Tudor Ashridge in

172. Harlaxton Manor, Lincolnshire, 1881. The cedar and stucco staircase, *c.* 1850. The spectacular Baroque decorations on the interior of Harlaxton were added by William Burn, who took over when Anthony Salvin retired.

Hertfordshire, and in 1816 William Wilkins had designed a splendid reproduction of an Elizabethan house at Tregothnan in Cornwall. But the first massive 'prodigy house' was Harlaxton Manor in Lincolnshire, which was designed by Salvin for Gregory de Ligne Gregory in 1831. The overwhelming exterior is like an enlarged and complicated version of Burghley with a few Baroque decorations thrown in here and there, but the interior, by William Burn, moves forward entirely into the late seventeenth century and is all outrageously Baroque, with an astonishing over-decorated staircase hall.

The combination of the two most exuberant styles, Elizabethan Renaissance and Baroque, did not appeal to other clients. The many reproductions of 'prodigy houses' which Burn later designed, such as Stoke Rochford, also in Lincolnshire, were more restrained and more faithfully Elizabethan, and so too were Salvin's, although one of them, Thoresby Hall, in Nottinghamshire, was even larger than Harlaxton.

173. Harlaxton Manor. Anthony Salvin's remarkable house, designed six years before the accession of Queen Victoria, has none of the clumsiness of many later Elizabethan Revival houses, such as Bear Wood.

Like Harlaxton, many of the new houses in the Elizabethan style were reminiscent of some of the originals. Two in particular resembled Wollaton, although they were closer to Smythson's ingenious plan than Willoughby's extraordinary decorations. One was Highclere Castle in Hampshire, where Sir Charles Barry remodelled a Georgian house for the Earl of Carnarvon in 1840 without altering the shape of the outer walls. And the other was Mentmore Towers in Buckinghamshire, designed by Sir Joseph Paxton and G. H. Stokes in 1851 for a banker, Baron Meyer Amschel de Rothschild, who imported seventeenth-century chimneypieces and furniture from France.

By the 1870s, when the agricultural economy was declining and few landed families were building, the Elizabethan style had overtaken Gothic in popularity. But these were not the only styles for large and extravagant country houses. There was also a considerable fashion for houses in a Picturesque Italianate style, a large number of which were designed by Sir Charles Barry. Barry's Italianate houses ranged from huge villas, such as Walton House in Surrey, which he designed for the Earl of Tankerville in 1835, to massive Renaissance palaces like Trentham Hall in Staffordshire and Cliveden House in Buckinghamshire, which he designed in 1840 and 1850 for the Duke of Sutherland. Like many of Barry's houses, these three were the result of the remodelling or rebuilding of earlier houses, and in some cases, as at Highclere, he managed to create an Italianate house without altering the original shell. His worst sacrilege in this field was at Kingston Lacey in Dorset. Apart from Coleshill, this was the only house by Sir Roger Pratt still standing, but after its encounter with Barry, the beautiful house was heartbreakingly disfigured.

This Italianate style was as close as the great Victorian houses came to the Classical tradition. But some of them came extremely close. Prestwold Hall in Leicestershire, which William Burn remodelled for Charles William Packe in 1842, had Classical façades and a Greek porch, and unlike Barry's houses it did not have a tower. There was even one Classical house with a symmetrical rectangular main block, Brodsworth Hall in Yorkshire, which was designed by an Italian, the Chevalier Casentini, and finished in 1870 under the direction of Philip Wilkinson for Charles Sabine Thellusson, the great-grandson of a Swiss banker who had just inherited a disappointingly small fortune after sixty-three years of notorious litigation. Like many large Victorian houses, Brodsworth had its entrance at one end, but, apart from its Classicism, there was also a more practical way in which it was different from all of

174. Brodsworth Hall, Yorkshire, 1861. An unusually symmetrical and Classical Victorian house, designed by an Italian, the Chevalier Casentini.

them. Instead of being far out in the servants' wing, so that the family and their guests would not have to suffer the smells of cooking, the kitchen at Brodsworth was in the main body of the house, on the other side of the corridor from the dining-room.

And there was yet another popular style. A number of the *nouveaux riches,* eager to build as grandly as possible and in some cases inspired by the new hotels in London, commissioned architects to design French châteaux for them. One of the earliest was Château Impney in Worcestershire, which was designed in 1869 for an industrialist, John Corbett, by a French architect, Auguste Tronquois. During the following two years, Sir Charles Barry's third son, E. M. Barry, who had designed two of the London hotels, designed three châteaux – Chobham Park and Shabden in Surrey for a brewer and a London merchant, C. J. F. Comb and J. Cattley, and Wykehurst Park in Sussex for Henry Huth, the son of a banker. But

175. Waddesdon Manor, Buckinghamshire, 1874. Baron Ferdinand de Rothschild brought over a French architect, G. H. Destailleur, to design his château and imported eighteenth-century French panelling for many of its rooms, together with a magnificent collection of eighteenth-century French furniture.

the grandest of them all was Waddesdon Manor in Buckinghamshire, which was designed in 1874 for Baron Ferdinand de Rothschild by another French architect, Gabriel-Hyppolyte Destailleur. The baron, whose money was not particularly new, built a menagerie and an aviary as well and planted the park with fully grown trees. When Gladstone's daughter Mary saw the house in 1885, she wrote afterwards in her diary, 'Felt much oppressed with the extreme gorgeousness and luxury . . . but there is not a book in the house save twenty improper French novels.'

The châteaux had little influence on the design of smaller houses, but the Gothic and Italianate styles were equally popular for the detached residences large enough for a family and six servants which the speculators were building in every suburb and the growing, prosperous and powerful middle classes were buying with the help of the new building societies. Until the middle of the nineteenth century most of the smaller Gothic houses were still stuccoed and built in the Regency tradition; after that, however, Pugin prevailed. Pugin set the example with his own houses, St Mary's Grange

at Alderbury in Wiltshire, which he completed in 1836, and The Grange at Ramsgate in Kent, which he completed eight years later; and his influence was carried into almost every town by the architects who designed not only the new churches but also the vicarages that went with them.

One of the most prolific of these architects was William Butterfield, who also designed one large and depressing house, Milton Ernest Hall in Bedfordshire. His vicarages, which were typical, were more restrained than Milton Ernest but similarly sombre, and for a while most of the middle-class Gothic houses were the same. During the last thirty years of the century, however, rich professionals and 'intellectuals' were building much more elaborate and pretentious Gothic houses, such as those that can still be seen in north Oxford or Hampstead.

176. Houses in Norham Gardens, Oxford, *c.* 1865. A mid-Victorian estate which was laid out by William Wilkinson, who also designed a number of the houses.

177. St Saviour's Vicarage, Coalpit Heath, Gloucestershire, 1845. 'In many ways the house is more important historically than the castles of Salvin, the palaces of Barry and the manor houses of Pugin.' Despite its Gothic details, this vicarage, designed by William Butterfield, is the first example of the Vernacular Revival style.

178. St Mary's Grange, Wiltshire, 1835. A. W. Pugin designed this house for himself, although he only lived in it for two years. So great was his devotion to the Middle Ages that he even had a garderobe leading off his bedroom.

The Italianate style, which evolved in smaller houses from the detached and semi-detached villas of John Nash, became increasingly popular after 1848, when the Prince Consort completed the Italianate Osborne House on the Isle of Wight, and, to the dismay of many, faced it in stucco. In the middle of the century, most of the rows of identical detached houses in the suburbs were stuccoed and Italianate, but by the 1870s even the speculators had succumbed to the influence of Pugin and were building rows of Gothic houses instead.

179. Osborne House, Isle of Wight, 1845. Queen Victoria and Prince Albert set their seal of approval on the Italianate style when they built their seaside retreat. Although designed by Thomas Cubitt, it owes much in style to Sir Charles Barry, whose Italianate houses were derived from Nash's villas. Osborne's influence even crossed the Atlantic.

In terraces, the Classical Georgian style survived well past the middle of the century, although it often acquired heavy stucco decorations around the windows. But inevitably the number of Gothic terraces increased steadily, and there were even a few Tudor terraces, such as those in Lonsdale Square in London, which were designed as early as 1838 by R. C. Carpenter. Despite the fact that they continued with a Georgian style, however, the early Victorian speculative builders did not follow the geometrical lay-out of the Georgian developments. Influenced by their Picturesque Italianate architecture, they also chose irregular Picturesque plans. In London's Ladbroke Grove and Holland Park, for example, the streets, squares and terraces meet each other at different angles and twist round the contours of the hills, and the houses, which were built at different times, vary considerably. In one street there can be Classical terraces on one side and Italianate semi-detached villas on the other.

The architects of the nineteenth century were the first who had to contend with the added difficulty of supplying their houses with 'services', but the new inventions of the industrial age were surprisingly slow in finding their way into private houses. In 1787, only a few years after the introduction of the first efficient and smokeless oil lamp, the Argand Lamp, Lord Dundonald lit the hall of Dundonald Abbey in Scotland with gas. In 1813 the London and Westminster Gas Company was founded, and by 1823, when gas lighting was introduced in Bristol, the London company had expanded to become the Gas, Light and Coke Company, with several manufacturing stations supplying 122 miles of street mains. But the gas was extremely expensive and smelly and it was thought to be only fit for lighting streets and public buildings. It was not until the 1850s, with the introduction of regenerative burners, that gas became more efficient and economical. After that, several of the large country houses, such as Kelham, were built with their own gas works, and during the 1860s gas works were built to supply both houses and streets in almost every large town and city. At the same time, however, the cheap and odourless American Kerosene was introduced. At the end of the century there were still many town houses and a few large country houses which were only lit by Kerosene oil lamps.

Victorian houses heated their water with coal-burning boilers and their rooms with coal fires, shrouding the cities in sinister and unhealthy smog. Only a few of the large country houses had primitive central-heating systems, which consisted of hot air ducts connected to the boiler-room or hot water pipes with cumbersome radiators, but they were

180. Self-portrait by Daniel Maclise showing the artist working by the light from an oil lamp.

181. Westbourne Terrace, London, *c.* 1830. A street of grand houses which was part of the large development called Tyburnia by the Victorians. It was laid out in 1827.

183. Cottages in a nineteenth-century village.

182. Bluegate Fields, Stepney. Gas lamps in Victorian London's streets lit even the overcrowded slums.

seldom efficient and were never fitted in more than one or two of the ground-floor rooms. As time passed, more and more town houses were connected to water mains, and in the country houses the water was pumped by steam into tanks in towers, most of which were incorporated in the design of the house. Until the last quarter of the century, however, many large houses and almost all the smaller houses had no separate bathroom, and although water-closets became common, it was not until the 1880s, when gas cookers and even electricity were introduced, that a few houses were at last being fitted with ventilated drains.

The technical developments of the industrial society had no effect on the terrifying Victorian slums. Most industrialists built as cheaply as possible for their workers. Within a few years their new houses were as damp and insanitary as the Georgian versions. The lowest paid and the unemployed were crowded into crumbling tenements, and in 1851, out of a population of almost eighteen million, more than 10 per cent was homeless. In 1844 a Society was founded for Improving the Conditions of the Labouring Classes, but it had a long way to go and, despite the patronage of Prince Albert and Anthony Ashley Cooper, later Earl of Shaftesbury, it was at first met with frustrating indifference.

184. A typical Victorian drawing-room, *c*. 1860, lit by gas.

In the countryside, however, conditions were often better. A number of landlords built Picturesque cottages and villages for their labourers, if for no other reason than to improve the approaches to their mansions. Many were inevitably Gothic, but the local builders continued to build in their traditional styles, uninfluenced by the current fashions; and after the middle of the century some of the architects began to follow their example. In the 1850s William Butterfield designed simple brick cottages with gables at Baldersby St James in Yorkshire, and George Devey designed cottages in the local, tile-hung style at Penshurst in Kent. In the 1860s William Eden Nesfield designed half-timbered cottages at Hampton in Arden in Warwickshire and brick and tile-hung gabled cottages at Crewe Hall in Cheshire. And it was from these Picturesque versions of the traditional English cottage that new fashions for Vernacular architecture emerged.

185. Despite the picturesque exteriors of many nineteenth-century cottages, their interiors, which had brick or stone floors laid straight onto the ground, were damp, cold and ill lit.

CHAPTER 11

Return to the Vernacular

In 1856, while he was designing cottages at Penshurst for Lord De L'Isle and Dudley, George Devey designed two larger houses which were the precursors of the two most popular styles in the 'Vernacular Revival'.

The smaller of the two was Hammerfield, which he built on the Penshurst estate for James Nasmith, the inventor of the steam hammer. With its combination of brick, half-timbering and jettied gables, Hammerfield was the first house in the style that was later to be known as 'Old English'; and it was the prototype for the thousands of half-timbered suburban houses that were still being built long after the beginning of the twentieth century.

The other house, Betteshanger, near Deal, was originally a Georgian villa which had been bought by a friend of Nasmith, Sir Walter James, later Lord Northbourne, who was then living in a rented house near Penshurst. When Sir Walter commissioned him to rebuild the villa and enlarge it, Devey designed a huge rambling house in a mixture of styles and then built it in a variety of local materials, so that it would look as though it had grown up over the centuries. He even made up a history for it. According to the story, it had once been a medieval manor house, of which only the tower now survived. From time to time this tower had been repaired, and in the reign of Elizabeth I a large flint-and-stone wing with a Renaissance porch had been added to it. In the reign of James I a second and more impressive brick wing with Flemish gables had been built on, and a little brick gable with a window beneath it had been added in the side of the porch; and on the inside of this wing, during the eighteenth century, a staircase had been erected in the middle of the state apartments. The wings and the tower were completed by 1861, but Devey continued adding to them for another twenty years. Although much of Betteshanger was also 'Old English', the brick wing with Flemish gables contained most of the features of the style that was later to be known misleadingly as 'Queen Anne'.

Devey built many other houses in the 'Old English' style, including another in Kent, St Alban's Court, where he built most of the ground floor in stone and the rest in brick, to make it look as though a stone house had once been ruined and then rebuilt in brick to exactly the same design. But the 'Old

English' and 'Queen Anne' styles became fashionable through the houses of two other architects, William Eden Nesfield and Norman Shaw, the most influential architect of his generation.

Nesfield's 'Old English' houses were extremely restrained. In 1846 he designed the Gothic Cloverley Hall in Shropshire for J. P. Heywood, a Liverpool banker, and gave it no more than tall Elizabethan chimneys and a few 'Old English' decorations. But in the following year, for Henry Vallance, a London solicitor, he designed Farnham Park in Buckinghamshire with a small tower, tile-hung gables and wooden-framed windows.

Shaw, on the other hand, designed 'Old English' houses that were elaborate and spectacular. The house that really made 'Old English' fashionable was Leys Wood in Sussex, which Shaw designed in 1868 for J. W. Temple, managing director of the Shaw, Savill shipping line, which had been founded by Shaw's brother. Built in a mixture of styles from the fifteenth, sixteenth and seventeenth centuries, Leys Wood had a courtyard, a towered gatehouse and jettied, half-timbered gables. Following the example of Cloverley, the rooms were of different heights and set at different levels, and following Farnham, there was an inglenook in the dining-room. It was the first of the many houses that were to be described appropriately as 'quaint'.

186. Fanciful *Punch* cartoon of 1882, which has proved to be remarkably accurate.

THE COMING FORCE—MR. PUNCH'S DREAM.

Shaw's most spectacular house, however, was Cragside in Northumberland, which he designed in 1870 for William Armstrong, who was later to be created Baron Armstrong. Armstrong had started his working life as a solicitor, but in 1840 he had invented an improved hydraulic engine, and seven years later he had founded the Elswick Engineering Works, which were to bring him his first enormous fortune. In 1854, during the Crimean War, he had launched himself on the road to a second and even larger fortune with the invention of the Armstrong Gun, the first gun to be breach loading and fire shells instead of balls through a rifled barrel. When Cragside was completed in 1884, it contained hydraulic lifts, hydraulically powered central heating and hydraulic machines that turned the spit in the kitchen and moved the heavy pots in the conservatory. Since Armstrong had invented a turbine for producing electricity and was a friend of Sir Joseph Swan,

188. Cragside, Northumberland, 1870–84. Norman Shaw was commissioned to add on two rooms to Sir William Armstrong's shooting lodge at the end of 1869. During the next fifteen years the original small house steadily grew in size and complexity, and its once barren moorland site was transformed into a forest.

187. Contemporary engraving showing the newly invented electricity that was used at Cragside.

whose electric lamp had anticipated Edison's by twenty years, it was also the first house in England to have electric lighting; and it even had a telephone connected to the shooting lodge.

As its name suggests, Cragside was built on a site that was blasted out of the side of a gorge above the River Coquet. The house is half-hidden now by the trees that have grown up around it, but when it was built, unlike most large Victorian houses, it could be seen from many miles away. Like a romantic castle, it is a tight mass of blocks and towers in a variety of styles and materials, and as in all Shaw's large houses, some of the sections were designed to contain rooms which could be used by guests at weekend house parties and then ignored when only the family were at home. Its design is the epitome of the 'Old English' style, and its setting is one of the most romantic in England.

The earliest house in the style that was later to be known as 'Queen Anne' is a little lodge which Nesfield designed in Kew Gardens near London in 1867. With its steep roof, heavy chimney, dormer windows, decorated brickwork and white-painted window frames, it looks more like a Dutch house than anything that was built during the reign of Queen Anne. In the following year, Nesfield incorporated all these features in a large country house in North Wales, Kinmel Park, which he built for H. R. Hughes, who owned a copper mine in Anglesey, and in 1872 he incorporated Devey's Flemish gables in another Welsh house, Bodrhyddan in Flintshire. His most attractive 'Queen Anne' house, however, and the one which was to become the model for many others in the suburbs and home counties, was Loughton Hall in Essex, which he designed in 1878 for his cousin's brother-in-law, the Rev. J. W. Maitland.

Norman Shaw did not design any large country houses in the 'Queen Anne' style, but he was the leader among those who spread the fashion for it in London. In 1873, when he designed Lowther Lodge in Kensington Gore, now the head-quarters of the Royal Geographical Society, he made it a 'Queen Anne' house with differing gables set around an open courtyard. In 1875, however, when he designed Swan House in Chelsea Embankment, he added a few 'Old English' features as well. The first and second floors are jettied, and on the first floor there are three oriel windows which were copied from the early-seventeenth-century Sparrowe's House in Ipswich. Shaw used these windows again in the same year on his own house in Ellerdale Road, Hampstead, and they were soon being copied elsewhere.

Several other leading architects also designed large 'Queen

189. 5 and 7 Cadogan Gardens, London, 1892. Designed by F. G. Knight for rich clients, these town houses combine features of the 'Queen Anne' style with 'Dutch' gables. The result provides a good example of architectural confusion.

No. 5 & 7
Cadogan Gardens. S.W.

Fred. C. Knight Archt.

Second Floor Plan
- Bed Rm
- Dress Rm
- area
- Bath Rm
- Bed Rm
- Dress Rm

First Floor Plan
- Boudoir
- area
- Landing
- Drawing Rm

Ground Floor Plan
- Stables
- Dining Rm
- area
- Hall
- Morning Rm

Anne' houses in London, some of which were built before any of Shaw's. As early as 1868, when Nesfield was designing Kinmel Park, Philip Webb used many of the 'Queen Anne' features on the house that he designed for the Hon. George Howard, 1 Palace Green, although he also gave it Gothic arches. In 1871, J. J. Stevenson built himself a house in the 'Queen Anne' style which is now 140 Bayswater Road. And the partnership of Sir Ernest George and Harold Peto built an impressive row of elaborately Flemish houses with mullioned windows in Harrington Gardens during the 1880s, one of which was the London home of the librettist W. S. Gilbert. On a smaller scale, there is even one development, around Cadogan Square, Pont Street and Sloane Street, which contains houses designed by all these architects, including Shaw, who designed three in Cadogan Square.

Despite the large numbers of Gothic town houses which were still being built, the 'Queen Anne' style became so popular with the professional classes and the 'artistic community' that in 1875, shortly after the opening of Turnham Green railway station on the outskirts of London beyond Hammersmith, a cloth merchant called Jonathan Carr bought forty-five acres close to the station and began to develop them entirely with 'Queen Anne' houses. The result was Bedford Park, one of the earliest garden suburbs in England. Carr engaged Norman Shaw to plan the estate, but Shaw only designed a few of the houses, together with the pub, the church and a shop. The others were designed by architects who were prepared to follow his example.

By 1881 Carr had built almost five hundred 'quaint' 'Queen Anne' houses on his forty-five acres. They varied in size; some were detached, some semi-detached and some in terraces, but each one had its own garden, and they were all brick with steep roofs, gables, heavy chimneys, white-painted woodwork and small window panes. Carr also built a kindergarten, a day school, an art school, tennis courts and a club house; and within a few years, his residents, who paid rents of between £30 and £130 a year, had started an amateur dramatic society, a ladies' discussion group, a vigilance committee and a voluntary fire brigade.

When he advertised the estate in 1881, Carr proclaimed: 'A Garden and a Bath Room with hot and cold water to every house, whatever its size.' At the top of his advertisement he also announced that 'The Estate is built on gravelly soil and has the most approved sanitary arrangements' and that the annual death rate was under six per thousand. With their bathrooms and approved sanitation, his houses were as modern as he

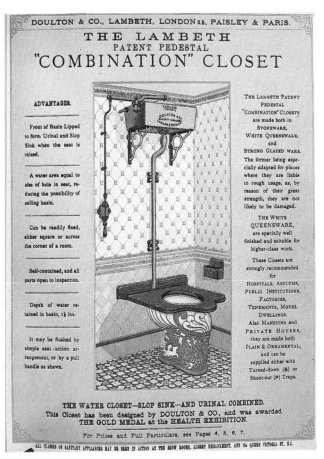

190. Bedford Park, London, 1875. The first garden suburb was laid out by Norman Shaw. Shaw also designed a few of the houses and others were designed by his protegés.

191. Advertisement for a water-closet.

could make them – but he had built them just a little too soon. In the same year, 1881, S. Stevens Hellyer, the head of an old-established firm of London plumbers, gave a series of lectures at the Society of Arts, in which he described a newly developed system of sanitation which included ventilated drains.

The pub and many of the houses in Bedford Park, including Carr's, were decorated with tiles and wallpapers which had been designed by the poet and artist William Morris. Morris was the leading light in the new Arts and Crafts Movement. A follower of Pugin and Ruskin, he admired the Middle Ages, and he detested the clutter of Victorian rooms and the mass-produced furniture and ornaments of the industrial age. He

GLEDHOW HALL. LEEDS.
J. Kitson Jun.ʳ Esqʳˢ
BATH-ROOM in BURMANTOFT FAIENCE.
Messʳˢ Chorley and Connon.
Architects.
Wyman & Sons Photo-Litho

192. Design for a tiled bathroom.

193. Standen, Sussex, 1891. The central section of Webb's house containing the drawing-room and dining-room is arranged symmetrically and can be called 'Queen Anne' with more justification than the rest of the house or many others in the same style. Webb used traditional materials, although, like many architects at this time, he was not averse to using a wide range of different materials.

believed that a room should be simply furnished and that a house should contain nothing that was not beautiful or useful, and through the success of his firm, Morris, Marshall, Faulkner and Co., which sold wallpapers, furniture, textiles, carpets and many other products, all of which had been designed and handmade by craftsmen, he was now changing the attitude of the English middle classes towards interior decor. But more than twenty years earlier, shortly before he started his company with Philip Webb and some of the leading pre-Raphaelite painters, Morris had also been responsible for the introduction of the most simple of the styles in the Vernacular Revival. In 1856, while he was at Oxford, he had become a pupil in the offices of the Gothic architect G. E. Street. It was there that he had met Philip Webb, who was then Street's chief assistant, and in 1859 he had invited Webb to design a house for him.

Many of Webb's later country houses, such as Standen in Sussex and Smeaton Manor in Yorkshire, were in a very idiosyncratic version of the 'Queen Anne' style, and in 1879 he designed one huge and uniquely simple mansion, Clouds in Wiltshire, which its owner, Percy Wyndham, described as the

'house of the age'. But as a young man Webb had been a follower of the Gothic school, and he admired the simple vicarages of Street and Butterfield. In designing The Red House at Bexley Heath in Kent for William Morris, he applied their principles and his own imagination to creating a simple English 'farmhouse' out of local materials.

Although Webb did not continue to design entirely in the style of The Red House, there were several who followed his example. The most eminent was Charles Annesley Voysey, who had been an assistant to George Devey and was also a member of the Arts and Crafts Movement. Like some of the eighteenth-century architects, Voysey designed every detail of his houses, including the furniture; but unlike them he derived his style from English sources. His houses are built in the same materials as farmhouses; they have bay windows and often sloping buttresses, and their brick or rough-cast walls are always painted white. Of the many that he built in the home counties around London, one of the finest is his own house, The Orchard at Chorleywood in Hertfordshire, but there are good examples elsewhere as well, such as Broadleys and Moor Crag on Lake Windermere. In 1891 he designed a house in Bedford Park, 14 South Parade, which, despite its white walls and modernity, contrasts surprisingly well with its 'quaint' brick neighbours, and in 1899 he designed Spade House at Sandgate in Kent for the novelist H. G. Wells.

Two other contemporaries of Voysey who followed in the same tradition were M. H. Baillie Scott, who designed cottage-style houses such as the White Lodge at Wantage in Berkshire, and Ernest Newton, who designed less imaginative houses, such as Red Court at Haslemere in Surrey. The carefully simple houses which Voysey and these two designed at the end of the nineteenth century seem unexceptional today, but that may only be because they were the models for the many thousands of clumsy copies that were built during the 1930s in the suburbs of almost every English city and several in Europe as well.

Webb's tradition continued further into the twentieth century in the designs of two architects who had both worked in the office of Sir Ernest George and Harold Peto. One was Sir Guy Dawber, founder of the Council for the Preservation of Rural England, who designed houses in a style that followed from Newton's, such as Stowell Hill in Somerset, Burdocks in Gloucestershire or Wiveton Hall in Norfolk. And the other, and the most famous of them all, was Sir Edwin Lutyens.

Although he was to design in a variety of styles, Lutyens started in the Vernacular tradition. In 1890, at the age of

194. The Red House, Bexley Heath, Kent, 1859. Influenced by the vicarages of G. E. Street and William Butterfield, the revolutionary house that Philip Webb designed for William Morris was in turn to influence many of the Vernacular Revival houses that followed it.

195. Munstead Wood, Surrey, 1896. Edwin Lutyens designed this house for his life-long friend Gertrude Jekyll, the great gardener. Here Lutyens was building in the first and possibly most successful of all his styles – the 'Surrey cottage' style.

255

twenty, he abandoned his articled pupillage in the office of George and Peto to set up on his own, and in 1896 he received his first important commission. It was to design Munstead Wood at Godalming in Surrey for the famous gardener Gertrude Jekyll. Built in stone with a tiled roof, heavy clusters of brick chimneys and a medieval atmosphere, Munstead Wood was the first of Lutyens's so-called 'Surrey houses', which were set in romantic gardens designed by Gertrude Jekyll. One of the finest is Deanery Gardens at Sonning in Berkshire, which he designed in 1899 for Edward Hudson, the proprietor of *Country Life* magazine. In the same year, however, he also designed Tigbourne Court at Hambledon in Surrey for Sir Edgar Horne. Tigbourne is much larger than his earlier houses. It is a dramatic and imaginative modern interpretation of an Elizabethan house, with a gabled central block, a loggia and tall chimneys towering over its wings, but it also contains a foretaste of the houses that Lutyens was soon to design. Its symmetry is almost Classical, and in the movement of its wings and the curving sweep of the walls beside them there is more than a hint of the Baroque.

Towards the end of Queen Victoria's reign, the tastes of some architects and their patrons were turning towards the styles of the Georgian and Regency periods. The affection for castles had never quite died: in 1878 Norman Shaw rebuilt the castle at Flete in Devon for H. B. Mildmay, who had inherited a fortune from his mother, a member of the Baring banking family. But in general the trend was towards Classical architecture. In 1872 two amateur architects, Wilfrid and Lady Anne Blunt, who were friends of Philip Webb and William Morris, led the way with the neo-Georgian Crabbet Park in Sussex. After that some 'Queen Anne' houses, such as Shaw's 170 Queen's Gate, London, acquired more Classical proportions and became more obviously 'Queen Anne' rather than Flemish. There was a considerable Georgian influence in Webb's Smeaton Manor, and in 1890 Shaw designed the entirely Classical Bryanston in Dorset for Lord Portman. It was this neo-Georgian tradition that Lutyens was to follow in his later work, although he did have more Picturesque excursions as well. In 1903 he rebuilt Lindisfarne Castle on Holy Island off the coast of Northumberland, and in 1910 he designed the awesome granite Castle Drogo in Devon.

Heathcote, at Ilkley in West Yorkshire, which he designed in 1906, is Lutyens's only Baroque country house. His other Classical houses, such as Great Maytham and The Salutation in Kent, or Nashdown Abbey in Buckinghamshire, are more strictly neo-Georgian. But at one house, Gledstone Hall in

196. 170 Queen's Gate, London, 1887. The exterior and interior of Norman Shaw's most restrained house.

SPADE HOVSE SANDGATE KENT FOR H.G.WELLS ESQ

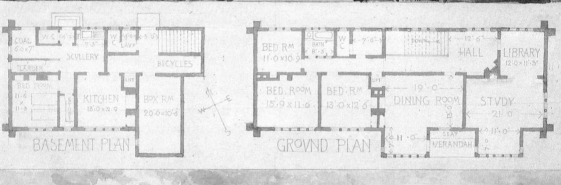

BASEMENT PLAN

COAL 6'0"x7'
W.C 7'3"
SCVLLERY
LARDER
BED ROOM 11'6" 11'3"
KITCHEN 18'0"x12'9"
W.C LAV?
K·6·0?
BICYCLES
LIFT
BOX RM 20'6"x10'6"

GROVND PLAN

BED RM 11'0"x10'5"
BATH 8'3"
W.C 7'6"
DOWN
12'6"
HALL
LIBRARY 12'0"x11'3"
BED ROOM 15'9"x11'0"
BED RM 13'0"x12'6"
LIFT
19'0"
DINING ROOM
STVDY 21'0"
SEAT VERANDAH
11'0"

197. (*Left*) Spade House, Sandgate, Kent, 1900. The house was built to the third design which Charles Voysey submitted to H. G. Wells. Four years later, Voysey added a further storey to what was intended to be a bungalow, with a lower floor for the kitchens under part of the house. The rendered and white-painted walls of Voysey's houses were a deliberate protest against the almost universal use of brick.

198. (*Right*) Pre-First World War London underground poster. When the bus and underground systems developed in the twentieth century, the speculative builders turned to Voysey's houses as models for their new suburban developments and produced scaled-down and debased versions.

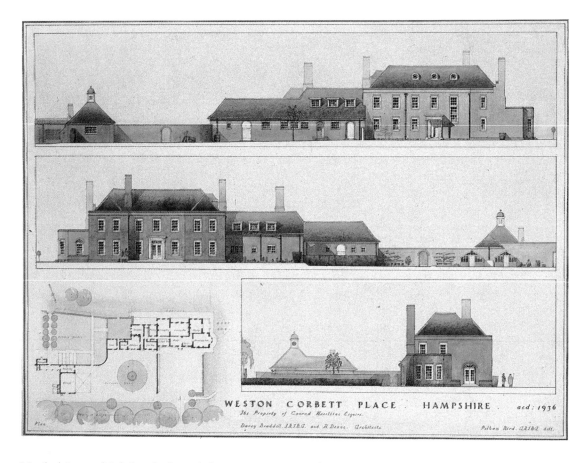

WESTON CORBETT PLACE . HAMPSHIRE . *acd : 1936*
The Property of Conrad Hamilton Esquire.
Darcy Braddell F.R.I.B.A. and H.Deane Architects
Pelham Bird A.R.I.B.A. del.

Yorkshire, which he designed for a cotton manufacturer, Sir Amos Nelson, in 1923, he mixed Palladian proportions with a neo-Classical portico and a Vernacular roof.

Lutyens's last large country house was Middleton Park in Oxfordshire, which he designed for the Earl of Jersey in 1935. By then the large country house was very different from those of the previous century. Middleton had no need for its own laundry, but it had fourteen bathrooms, garaging for fifteen cars and a row of separate houses for servants. But by then the large country house was itself an anachronism, and although the neo-Georgian style was still popular, the International Style of Modern architecture had arrived. In the same year, for instance, E. Maxwell Fry was designing the concrete and steel Sun House in Frognal Way, Hampstead.

The European version of the new functional and geometric domestic architecture, which had evolved in Germany and France in the work of Walter Gropius and Le Corbusier, reached England in 1925 when the German architect Peter Behrens designed New Ways, 508 Wellingborough Road,

199. Weston Corbett Place, Hampshire, 1936. The new International Style, imported from Europe, had little appeal for most English clients. Architects like Darcy Braddell and Humphrey Deane had flourishing practices producing neo-Georgian designs such as Weston Corbett.

201. Bentley's, Halland, Sussex. Serge Chermayeff designed this house in 1934 for himself. Unlike virtually all the other pre-war houses designed in the International Style, Bentley's has not dated – it could well have been designed last year.

Northampton, for the engineer W. J. Basset-Lowke. During the 1930s, when the Nazis were suppressing Modern architecture, several of the leading German architects came to England, including Gropius himself, but they found few clients and soon moved on to the United States. Nevertheless, there were more than fifty 'Modern' houses built in England before the Second World War. The earliest in the International Style after New Ways was High and Over at Amersham in Buckinghamshire, which was designed in 1928 by Amyas Connell. There is one in London which Gropius designed with Fry in 1936, 66 Old Church Street, Chelsea; and there are several others in London by architects who were later to become distinguished, such as 32 Newton Road, which was designed by Sir Denys Lasdun in 1938.

But at the same time there were some architects who were using the style with traditional local materials. In 1935, for example, Mary Crowley used brick at Tewin in Hertfordshire, and in 1938 Connell used timber at Potcroft in Sutton, West Sussex. Just at the moment when war brought an end to domestic building, an English version of the International Style was emerging.

200. (*Above*) New Ways, Wellingborough Road, Northampton, 1925. The first house in England to be designed in the International Style and appropriately designed by the German architect Peter Behrens.

202. A mid-nineteenth-century
view of very basic sanitation.

CHAPTER 12

Towns and Suburbs

IN 1837, the year in which Charles Dickens published the first episodes of *Oliver Twist,* there were over forty thousand children under the age of sixteen living in England's workhouses. Known as 'Poor Law Bastilles', the workhouses had proliferated after the Poor Law Amendment Act of 1835, but their humiliating shelter, in which husbands, wives and children were separated, was denied to all but the destitute, and their discipline was designed to deter applicants. The Act had been passed in an attempt to limit the burden of the poor on parishes. For the poor who could avoid the workhouses, conditions were often, if anything, worse. Many of the back-to-back houses in the industrial cities contained more than one family, and the migratory inhabitants of the city tenements were sleeping more than two to a bed. Forty thousand people in Manchester and Liverpool – over 20 per cent of their populations – were living in dark, damp basements which were often flooded with the contents of unemptied cesspits. In one street in Manchester, Parliament Street, 380 people shared one privy.

Yet the reason for so much poverty was also the reason why the towns were not so crowded as they were soon to become. Back at the beginning of Queen Victoria's reign there was no sign and little hope that the depression was about to end. In Manchester 116 mills were idle, and trade had come to such a standstill in Stockport that the town was cynically described as 'To Let'. Unemployment and hunger were widespread, and inevitably they led to feeble and ill-organised rioting.

The government's immediate and totally effective response to the civil unrest was to dispatch troops to all the major industrial towns, but during the 1840s it also attempted to improve the conditions of the 'labouring classes'. As a result of Edwin Chadwick's report on sanitation, the Public Health Act of 1848 imposed the responsibility for providing effective drains and sewers on the new borough councils, which had been established by the Municipal Corporations Act of 1835. In a series of Factory Acts, the first of which had been passed in 1833, Anthony Ashley Cooper and others succeeded in banning the employment of children under nine and limiting the working hours of women and young persons to ten and a half per day, which effectively limited the men's hours as well,

since they could not work without the others. In 1851, the year in which he succeeded to the earldom of Shaftesbury, Ashley Cooper attempted to control conditions in the tenements with the first of his Common Lodging Houses Acts. But his inspectors had an impossible task: as a result of the already reviving economy, more people than ever before were moving to the towns in search of work. Within six years the country's trading income had doubled, and so too had the population of the tenements.

Despite the government's efforts to provide better sanitation and to improve conditions in factories and tenements, any attempts to provide better housing were left entirely to charities and philanthropic employers. In London the members of the Society for Improving the Conditions of the Labouring Classes managed to raise a small amount of money quite quickly, not in charitable donations but in capital investments, on which they paid a modest return of around 5 per cent per annum. In 1845 they built a few houses in Clerkenwell, including small lodging houses. Soon afterwards they built larger lodging houses with cubicled dormitories in George Street, St Giles, in the middle of the worst slum in London. And then, in 1849, they built a block of 'Model Houses for Families' in Streatham Street, Bloomsbury, to a design by Henry Roberts. The building is still standing and occupied, and the example that it set is still being followed. The 'houses' are in fact flats, laid out on five floors around three sides of a courtyard in a brick and stuccoed Classical block; and on the inside of the courtyard, Roberts built galleries around each floor so that every self-contained dwelling could have its own front door. Naturally, the flats have been remodelled since, but when they were built, each one contained one or two bedrooms, a living-room, a kitchen and its own water-closet, and at a time when the average skilled workman was earning eighteen shillings a week, they were let at a weekly rent of either two shillings or four shillings.

In 1851 the Society exhibited a block of four 'Prince Albert's Model Cottages' at the Great Exhibition, fifty-eight of which were later built near Windsor at the prince's expense. After that it concerned itself chiefly with the renovation of tenements, but by then several other charities were building in London, and their example was soon to be followed by a few individual philanthropists. One was Angela Burdett-Coutts, who had inherited a fortune from her banker grandfather, and who was later rewarded with a peerage. In 1857 she commissioned Henry Darbishire to design the Gothic Columbia

203. 'Model Houses for Families', Bloomsbury, London, 1849. Designed by Henry Roberts for the Society for Improving the Conditions of the Labouring Classes, this was the first block of flats in England with galleries which gave each flat its own front door.

204. A privy in the back yard of a London house. This earth-closet was only connected to the main drainage and water supply after the Second World War.

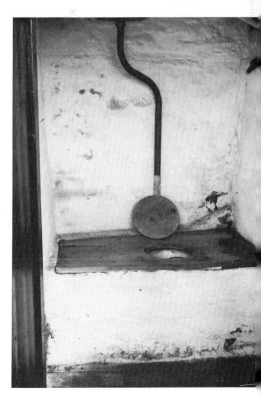

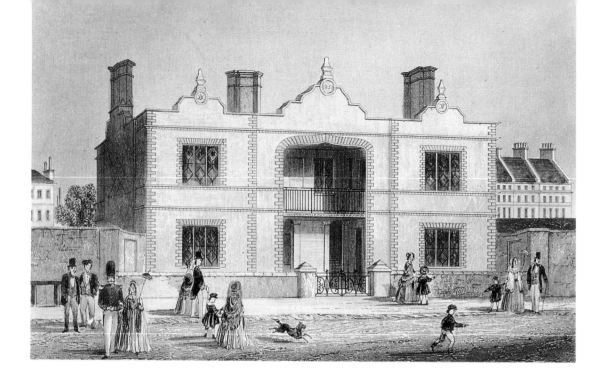

Square in Bethnal Green, and nine years later she commissioned him to design the elaborate Gothic market-place that she built beside it.

The most prolific charitable builder, however, was an American, George Peabody. Born in 1795 in South Danvers, Massachusetts, which was later renamed after him, Peabody became a partner in a Baltimore dry-goods store in 1829 and came to London in 1837 to establish himself as a leading merchant and banker. In 1862, with a capital of £150,000 which he later raised to £500,000, he founded the famous Peabody Trust. Like Angela Burdett-Coutts, he employed Darbishire as his architect, and in the following year they began to build the first of their many Italianate blocks, in Commercial Road, Spitalfields.

There are still a number of Peabody Buildings in London, such as those in Greenman Street, Islington, or Kemble Street, which runs into Drury Lane. Like most of the other charitable organisations, Peabody cleared slums in order to make room for his buildings, but their occupants were not the previous occupants of the slums. Although the rents were low, only skilled men with regular employment could afford them. The previous occupants had no choice but to swell the populations of the crowded slums elsewhere. For all their good intentions, the philanthropists and charities did nothing to house the most wretched of London's inhabitants, and they never had the capital to accommodate more than a tiny percentage of the skilled workforce.

In the industrial towns most of the employers and speculators continued to build as cheaply as possible. One of the earliest exceptions had been Richard Arkwright, who established the first water-powered cotton mill at Cromford in Derbyshire and built a row of 'model' houses for his workers in 1776; and it was also a mill-owner, Colonel Edward Akroyd, who was among the first Victorians to follow his example. The houses which Akroyd built for his workers at Copley outside Halifax in 1849 were only back-to-back terraces, although they were much better built than others and many of them had their own gardens, but ten years later he began to build a variety of Gothic houses on an estate nearby, which he called Akroydon. He chose the Gothic style because, as he said, 'This taste of our forefathers pleases the fancy, strengthens the house and home attachment, and entwines the present with memories of the past.' And he chose as his architect its leading exponent, George Gilbert Scott.

Scott planned the estate and designed the church, but unfortunately his designs for the houses proved too expensive,

205. Prince Albert's Model Lodging House, 1851, constructed in Hyde Park, together with his model cottages, for the Great Exhibition.

206. Peabody Estate, Clapham, London.

and they were eventually built to the designs of a local architect, W. H. Crossland. They were laid out in terraces, with yards at the rear which were separated from the yards of the next terrace by a lane. The smallest had a living-room, a kitchen and two bedrooms, and the larger gabled houses had a parlour and a third bedroom as well. Many of these larger houses were bought by the better-paid workers with money that they borrowed from building societies.

In 1864 Akroyd's great rivals in Halifax, the Crossley brothers, who manufactured carpets, began to build a similar estate at West Hill Park. But by the time work started at Akroydon there were already 150 workers' houses in Italianate terraces on an estate called Saltair outside the neighbouring town of Bradford. The builder of Saltair, Sir Titus Salt, who imported alpaca wool from South America, was even more ambitious than Akroyd or the Crossleys. He intended his estate to be 'a pattern to the country', and the local architects who designed his new mill, H. F. Lockwood and R. Mawson, continued to design houses for him over the next twenty years. By 1872 there were 820 houses in Saltair; there was a splendid park rising from the edge of the development to Ilkley Moor; and apart from a church and a chapel, it had shops, a school, a hospital, public baths and laundries, an institute that provided evening classes and forty-five alms-houses in which retired workers lived rent free on a pension of ten shillings a week.

Several other similar model housing schemes, such as the railway developments at Swindon and Derby, were begun soon after these. But there was also one small scheme which was different. In 1853 Price's Patent Candle Company began to build seventy-six houses at Bromborough Pool in the Wirral peninsular in Cheshire. The houses were either semi-detached or in terraces of four, and each one had a garden at the front and the rear. This was the example that was to be followed by the two most important and influential schemes, Port Sunlight and Bournville, which were built during the 1890s.

In 1888 the manufacturer of Sunlight Soap, William Lever, later Lord Leverhulme, moved his business from Warrington to a new factory on the Wirral beside the Mersey and laid out the avenues of Port Sunlight on 160 acres beside it. The 720 houses, many of which were designed by leading architects, including Sir Ernest George, are either semi-detached or in terraces of four or six. They are built in 'Old English' or Vernacular styles and in a variety of materials, and in the half-timbered houses, which follow the traditional Cheshire pat-

207. Cottages in Greendale Road, Port Sunlight, c. 1900. 'It is my and my brother's hope some day to build houses in which our workpeople will be able to live and be comfortable – semi-detached houses with gardens back and front in which they will be able to know more about the science of life than they can in a back-to-back slum, and in which they will learn that there is more enjoyment in life than the mere going to and returning from work and looking forward to Saturday night to draw their wages,' said William Lever at the inauguration ceremony for Port Sunlight. William Owen, the company architect, laid out the site, which remains one of the best planned developments of its kind.

terns, the half-timbering is part of the structure and not just a
Victorian façade. The smaller houses have a kitchen, a living-
room and three bedrooms, the larger have a parlour and a
fourth bedroom as well, and they were all built with a larder, a
bathroom and a separate internal water-closet. Lever endowed
the estate with the same amenities as Sir Titus had provided at
Saltair, but unlike Sir Titus, who prided himself on the
temperance of his workers, Lever trusted his employees
enough to include a fine village inn.

Bournville, which has now become a suburb of Birmingham, was planned by W. Alexander Harvey for George Cadbury, the chocolate manufacturer, in 1895. It is much larger than Port Sunlight. It covers a thousand acres and now contains about 2,500 houses, and from the outset their tenancies were not restricted to employees of Cadbury's company. It is also much less formally planned. But the houses are similar in size and are built in similar styles and groups, and those that copy the local Warwickshire half-timbering are among the most successful reproductions ever built.

Soon after work began at Bournville, another chocolate manufacturer, Joseph Rowntree, built a model village at New Earswick, outside York. But for this scheme Rowntree chose a pioneer as his architect, Raymond Unwin. Unwin, who was later to be knighted and become Chief Town Planning Officer at the Ministry of Health, expressed his views in a pamphlet, *Nothing Gained by Overcrowding*. He argued that most estates had a large number of superfluous roads and streets, and that if the space devoted to those were to be devoted to gardens instead, the same number of houses could be built at the same cost but with even larger open spaces between them. If the houses were to be arranged in *cul de sacs* around large open squares or circles, there would be no need for narrow-fronted terraces and all the limitations in internal plan which these entailed, and every house could have living-rooms with windows that caught the sunlight. At New Earswick Unwin put his ideas into practice and, in a style that followed Voysey's Vernacular, applied middle-class planning principles to broad-fronted working-class houses.

Unwin found an ally in Ebenezer Howard, who published *Garden Cities of Tomorrow* in 1902. Howard accepted that the model estates like New Earswick or Port Sunlight were an admirable alternative to the cheap, ill-built and tight-packed terraces with which the speculators had by now surrounded the industrial towns. But they were only extensions of the factories which they were built to serve. Howard wanted to build self-contained garden cities which would have their own civic centres, their own industries and no more than twelve houses per acre; and he believed that once such cities were built, they would create a demand for food in their own area which would revitalise the depressed agricultural economy. In 1903 he raised his capital on the stock exchange and commissioned Raymond Unwin and his partner Barry Parker to design Letchworth in Hertfordshire.

Letchworth, which now contains more than 5,000 houses,

208. Letchworth, Hertfordshire, 1903. The English were the pioneers of the garden city and Letchworth, designed by Raymond Unwin and Barry Parker for Ebenezer Howard, was the first.

was more of a social than an architectural success, and the formal civic centre was never completed. But both the architects and their promoter were to follow the experiment with schemes that were more architecturally ambitious. In 1906 Unwin and Parker began to build Hampstead Garden Suburb and engaged no less a man than Lutyens to design the formal and symmetrical Central Square. And in 1920 Howard commissioned a Frenchman, Louis de Soissons, to design Welwyn Garden City. At Welwyn, which is also in Hertfordshire, there is a much greater variety of styles than at Letchworth, and the houses range in size from large detached villas to little terraces of cottages.

210. Totterdown Fields, Tooting, London, 1903. London County Council's first suburban housing estate.

211. Albert Hall Mansions, London, 1879. The first block of mansion flats in London, designed by Norman Shaw.

In the 1870s the local authorities began to follow the examples of the charities and the philanthropic employers. One of the earliest was Liverpool, which started to build a tenement block called St Martin's Cottages in 1869. But like the speculators' terraces, or even the Peabody Buildings, the new council housing was at first only available to the better-paid artisans. In 1890, however, the Housing of the Working Classes Act gave Local Authorities the right to buy as much land as they needed for improvement schemes and obliged them to rehouse at least half the people who were left homeless as a result of any demolitions. Immediately the London County Council began to clear slums and replace them with simple Vernacular blocks of flats. In 1892 it built Beachcroft Buildings in Limehouse and the Boundary Estate at Bethnal Green, and in 1897 work started on the Millbank Estate in Westminster. But at the beginning of the twentieth century the Council decided to demolish some of the slums and rehouse their population elsewhere. As a result, in 1903, it built terraces of Vernacular cottages on its first suburban housing estate at Totterdown Fields in Tooting. Thereafter, London and the other cities divided their council housing between blocks of flats and suburban estates.

During the same period middle-class housing was similarly divided between blocks of flats and houses in the suburbs, although the middle classes at least had a choice. At first they regarded flats as beneath their dignity, but the idea became acceptable with the building of splendidly palatial blocks such as the 'Queen Anne' Albert Hall Mansions, which Norman Shaw designed in 1879, or the even more elaborate château-style Whitehall Court, which Thomas Archer and A. Green designed in 1884. During the twentieth century many equally palatial neo-Georgian blocks were built, and in the suburbs the speculators provided 'Old English' and Vernacular 'villas' with little change in their design other than the eventual addition of a garage and perhaps another bedroom above it. The only significant changes in the architecture of the middle-class suburbs came with the arrival of the neo-Georgian style and the bungalow.

The first building to be called a bungalow, after the *bangla* of Bengal, was built at Birchington in Kent in 1869. But for a while the bungalow was a rich man's retreat. It played the same role as the *cottage orné* had played during the Regency, and it was often equally picturesque, with a thatched roof and an Indian verandah. It was not until after the First World War that it found its way in a more sober guise into the suburbs.

During the 1930s, however, there were refreshing signs of

213. (*Above*) 'The Builders' by
Harry Bush, *c.* 1933.

212. Highpoint, Highgate,
1936–8. This high-rise
development, designed by
Bertholdt Lubetkin and the
Tecton group, is still one of the
very few that are sited in an
appropriate setting of lawns and
trees.

change, not only in the suburbs, but also in urban council
housing and in developments for industrial workers. The
influence of Modern architecture was not limited to men who
built houses for themselves. The Crittall Manufacturing
Company commissioned Burnet, Tait and Lorne to build
International Style houses for its disabled workers at Silver
End in Essex. The Russian-born Bertholdt Lubetkin and the
Tecton group designed the first blocks of high-rise flats in
Europe, Highpoint in Highgate, for an adventurous speculative investor. There is a large council housing scheme in
Ladbroke Grove, London, Kensal House, which looks as
though it was built during the 1950s, but which was in fact
built in 1939 to designs by Maxwell Fry, Robert Atkinson, C.
H. James and Grey Wornum. And these are only a few
examples. Before the Second World War broke out, the
architects of the Modern Movement had influenced every
sphere of domestic architecture.

Epilogue

OR the time being, Castle Drogo is the last castle to have been built in England. It is not, however, the last to have been built in Britain. In 1977 an architect, John Taylor, completed Castle Gyru in Wales to his own design. It may not be long before another follows it. The English are still building country houses, and for the most part, like the Victorians, they are building them in the styles of previous centuries.

Since the war the majority have been neo-Georgian, many of them built on the sites of earlier houses. The most prolific country-house architect, Claud Phillimore, has built forty neo-Georgian houses, and like most of his contemporaries and predecessors he has remodelled existing houses as well. But today remodelling can involve restoration. The survival of the Classical tradition has led to the redemption of a number of Victorian sins. One of the most satisfying rescues has been at Everingham Hall in Yorkshire, a house that belonged to the sixteenth Duke of Norfolk, for whom Phillimore designed the new Arundel Park in Sussex. Everingham had originally been a simple Classical house designed by John Carr of York, but it had been badly deformed by a Victorian grafting. In 1960 the duke commissioned Francis Johnson to restore it, and today it stands, not as a new house, but as John Carr's house reborn in all its former symmetry and proportion.

214. Arundel Park, Sussex, 1960. A neo-Georgian house designed by Claud Phillimore for the sixteenth Duke of Norfolk.

Among the neo-Georgians there are also committed and crusading Palladians. Until his death in 1973, the leader of the movement was Raymond Erith, and since then his place has been taken by his partner Quinlan Terry. One of the most famous post-war country houses, Kings Walden Bury in Hertfordshire, was designed by both of them for Sir Thomas Pilkington in 1967. In planning it they adhered so rigidly to Palladian principles that they even calculated the proportions by measuring them in fourteen-inch Venetian feet. Since its completion in 1971, more and more private clients have been commissioning purely Palladian houses; and although Castle Drogo has yet to be succeeded, the tradition of Mereworth and Chiswick continues. There is now another version of Palladio's Villa Capra, Henbury Hall in Cheshire, which was begun early in 1984 for Sebastian de Ferranti, to a design by Felix Kelly and Julian Bicknell.

There are, however, a number of private clients who have built modern country houses. The nearest in scale to the great houses of the past is the new Eaton Hall in Cheshire. The huge Gothic house designed by Alfred Waterhouse had been used by the army after the war for training National Service officers, and in 1961, after the War Office returned it to the Grosvenor Estate, the trustees of the Estate had decided to demolish it, imagining that no Duke of Westminster would ever want to live in it again. When the fifth duke succeeded to the title in 1967, all that remained was the chapel, the stables and the tall clock tower. But the new duke did want to live there, and he commissioned his brother-in-law John Dennys to replace Waterhouse's building with a Modern one.

The result, completed in 1973, is a large white symmetrical house in the tradition of Le Corbusier, with a swimming pool on the ground floor, the principal rooms on the first floor, and twelve bedrooms, seven bathrooms, two sitting-rooms and two dressing-rooms on the floor above. Unfortunately, despite its size, the house is dominated by the remains of Waterhouse's building beside it and the huge formal park and gardens in which it is set.

Two much more successful houses in the manner of the Modern Movement are the imposing Freechase in Sussex, clad in aluminium with stone-faced piers, which was designed for Sir Gawaine Baillie by Tom Hancock and Tony Swannell, and the long, low, concrete Thames House, which stands on the crest of a small hill in Berkshire and was designed for Timothy Sainsbury by Sir Denys Lasdun, the architect of the National Theatre.

Apart from Eaton Hall, there are several other Modern

country houses which have been built among the remains of the houses they replace. At Stratton Park in Hampshire, for example, the portico of George Dance Junior's neo-Classical house stands at the end of the Modern brick building like the hollow ruin of a Greek temple. But some builders have chosen to abandon the sites of earlier houses and start afresh elsewhere in their park; and one of these, Gerald Bentall, was also one of the few who followed in the footsteps of those great patrons of the past who commissioned such architects as Kent and Adam. When he began to build the new Witley Park in Surrey in 1961, he commissioned artists to design some of the decorative features, and he commissioned his architect, Patrick Gwynne, who had designed one of the best pre-war Modern houses, The Homewood in Surrey, to design most of the furniture as well.

But the men who build large houses no longer set the fashion for smaller houses, and surprisingly few of them have commissioned leading architects to design them. The successors to the great patrons of the past are now the Local Authorities.

When the Second World War ended, the Government and Local Authorities were presented with an enormous problem which was also a splendid opportunity. No new houses had been built in England for six years, and in the centres of the major industrial cities thousands had been destroyed by bombs. The Government made the money available and the Local Authorities set to work. The traditions of the past were set aside. In order to build the largest number of new homes as quickly as possible, there was no alternative but to use modern methods, and for these the only appropriate style was the Modern International Style. But there were very few building firms in England which had the expertise to work in steel and concrete. In the earliest of the new towns, such as Stevenage and Harlow, which were laid out in accordance with the precepts of Ebenezer Howard, nearly all the new houses were built in brick using traditional methods, even though most of them were Modern in design. It was in the centres of the cities that modern methods were used from the outset. As early as 1946, work had begun in London on the Hallfield Estate in Paddington, to designs by the Tecton group and the partnership of Drake and Lasdun, and on Churchill Gardens in Westminster, to designs by Powell and Moya.

With such a huge task in front of them, it was not long before some of the Local Authorities were setting up their own architects' offices. Inspired by Le Corbusier's ideal city, the London County Council office built the much-acclaimed

215. Flats at Roehampton, second phase, 1954–8. This large development of post-war rehousing was designed by the LCC's own architects' department. The late William Howell and C. St J. Wilson were responsible for the design of the second phase.

216. Hallfield Estate, Paddington, London, 1946. One of the first post-war developments in London, designed by the Tecton group and the partnership of Drake and Lasdun.

279

Roehampton scheme on the edge of Richmond Park between 1952 and 1959, with tower blocks of flats and lower terraces of maisonettes and two-storey houses set far apart in mature landscaped grounds which had once been the gardens of neighbouring villas. By the time the scheme was finished, many critics were complaining that there was no longer such a thing as an 'English' house. The new houses and blocks of flats were no different from those in Belgium, Germany or France. But by then their criticism was not entirely justified. In 1954 at Ham Common, and again in 1957 at Blackheath, on some of the few private developments that were not still neo-Georgian, Eric Lyons had designed simple Modern houses using brick and clapboard and other traditional materials, and these examples were now being followed on some of the Local Authority estates.

In the centres of the cities there was inevitably too little room for the landscaping required by Le Corbusier's dream, and although some Authorities built high-density housing schemes, the Government encouraged them to build high-rise flats instead by offering larger subsidies to those who did. During the 1950s and early 1960s, high-rise blocks of flats multiplied in scores of different concrete building systems, many of which had not been properly tested first. A number of these blocks were fine examples of monumental Modern architecture, but their scale was overwhelming and few people lived in them willingly. Many of them were set too close together, their environments were often desolate and some Authorities spent too little on maintenance. They were isolating for the elderly and miserable for families whose small children had nowhere to play within sight of their parents. In one or two areas of high unemployment they created as many social problems as they cured. The growing public opposition reached its climax in 1968 when part of a system-built tower block in London, Ronan Point, collapsed after a gas explosion. After that the high-rise flats fell from fashion with the Government and the Authorities, and within ten years the first of several blocks was being demolished.

Unfortunately there was no chance to start again. During the 1970s the money ran out. Strict controls on public-sector borrowing meant that many Authorities spent such resources as they had on reconditioning old houses. But in the few houses that are now being built there are signs that a new style is emerging. In an attempt to create houses that will be more attractive to their occupants and blend with the older houses around them, architects have fused the Modern and the Vernacular, designing brick terraces with irregular shapes and

217. Milton Keynes, 1967– . One of the last and probably the most thriving of the New Towns established after the war. Many of the earlier towns suffered as a result of being sited too close to London or other great cities, which deprived them of the opportunity to develop any individuality.

steep sloping roofs. The critics are still dissatisfied, maintaining that these houses are no more than continuations of the pre-war Vernacular tradition and that they are almost as monotonous as the Modern terraces of the 1950s and 1960s. But they are no more monotonous than the cramped Victorian and Edwardian terraces which they replace. They are much more comfortable and better built, and in a hundred years or so those that are still standing will be just as much a mirror of their times.

It has to be admitted, however, that there is very little contemporary domestic architecture in England which can compare with many of its Modern public and university buildings. But the architects can only design the houses that their clients commission. The Local Authorities are now restrained by cost, the private developers, on the whole, by caution, and most of the individual private clients by conservatism. Nevertheless, it will be difficult to remain unimaginative for long in a small country with a rich architectural heritage. There is still so much to live up to. Perhaps that is why so many private clients have taken refuge in 'The Rule of Taste'. It is easier to follow the best from the past than to rise to its challenge and match it or better it. Wherever they build, they are not too far from houses with symmetry and proportion, or perhaps even houses with porticos and pavilions. Inigo Jones is always watching.

Select Bibliography

Adam, Robert and James,
  The Works in Architecture of Robert and James Adam, ed. Robert Oresko
  (Academy Editions, 1975).
Airs, Malcolm,
  The Buildings of Britain: Tudor and Jacobean
  (Barrie and Jenkins, 1982).
Armstrong, J.R.,
  Traditional Buildings
  (E P Publishing, 1979).
Braun, Hugh,
  A Short History of English Architecture
  (Faber, 1978).
Brunskill, R. W.,
  Illustrated Handbook of Vernacular Architecture
  (Faber, 1978).
Cook, Olive,
  The English Country House
  (Thames and Hudson, 1984).
  The English House Through Seven Centuries
  (Penguin, 1984).
Davis, Terence,
  The Architecture of John Nash
  (Studio Vista, 1960).
Dixon, Roger, and Muthesius, Stefan,
  Victorian Architecture
  (Thames and Hudson, 1978).
Downes, Kerry,
  Vanbrugh
  (A. Zwemmer, 1977).
Fedden, Robin, and Browne, John Kenworthy,
  The Country House Guide
  (Jonathan Cape, 1979).
Girouard, Mark,
  Robert Smythson and the Architecture of the Elizabethan Era
  (Country Life, 1966).
  The Victorian Country House
  (Oxford, 1971).
  Sweetness and Light: The 'Queen Anne' Movement, 1860–1900
  (Oxford, 1977).
  Life in the English Country House
  (Penguin, 1980).
Guinness, Desmond, and Sadler Jr, Julius Trousdale,
  The Palladian Style in England, Ireland and America
  (Thames and Hudson, 1976).
Hill, Oliver, and Cornforth, John,
  English Country Houses: Caroline, 1625–1685
  (Country Life, 1966).

Hussey, Christopher,
  English Country Houses:
  (1) Early Georgian, 1715–60;
  (2) Mid Georgian, 1760–1800;
  (3) Late Georgian, 1800–40
  (Country Life, 1955–8).
Jones, Edward, and Woodward, Christopher,
  A Guide to the Architecture of London
  (Weidenfeld and Nicolson, 1983).
Kidson, Peter, Murray, Peter, and Thompson, Paul,
  A History of English Architecture
  (Pelican, 1979).
Lees-Milne, James,
  English Country Houses: Baroque, 1685–1715
  (Country Life, 1970).
  Tudor Renaissance
  (Batsford, 1951).
  The Age of Inigo Jones
  (Batsford, 1953).
  The Age of Adam
  (Batsford, 1947).
Lloyd, David,
  The Making of English Towns
  (Gollancz, 1984).
Lloyd, Nathaniel,
  A History of the English House
  (Architectural Press, 1975).
Mercer, Eric,
  English Vernacular Houses
  (H.M. Stationery Office, 1975).
Morris, Richard,
  The Buildings of Britain: Stuart and Baroque
  (Barrie and Jenkins, 1982).
The National Trust Atlas
  (The National Trust and George Philip and Son, 1984).
Richards, Sir James,
  The National Trust Book of English Architecture
  (The National Trust and Weidenfeld and Nicolson, 1981).
Richardson, Margaret,
  Architects of the Arts and Crafts Movement
  (Trefoil Books in association with the RIBA, 1981).
ROBINSON, JOHN MARTIN,
  The Latest Country Houses
  (The Bodley Head, 1984).
Strong, Sir Roy, Binney, Marcus, and Harris, John,
  The Destruction of the Country House
  (Thames and Hudson, 1974).
Summerson, Sir John,
  Architecture in Britain, 1530 to 1830
  (Penguin, 6th edition, 1977).
  Inigo Jones
  (Pelican, 1983).
Yarwood, Doreen,
  The Architecture of England
  (Batsford, 1967).

Watkin, David,
>   *The Buildings of Britain: Regency*
>   (Barrie and Jenkins, 1982).
Wittkower, Rudolf,
>   *Palladio and English Palladianism*
>   (Thames and Hudson, 1974).
Wood, Margaret,
>   *The English Mediaeval House*
>   (Phoenix House, 1965).
Woodforde, John,
>   *The Truth about Cottages*
>   (Routledge and Kegan Paul, 1984).

Index

Figures in italics indicate pages on which illustrations appear.